Can You Listen to a Woman

A Man's Journey to the Heart

OTHER TITLES FROM TIMELESS BOOKS

Kundalini Yoga for the West

Mantras: Words of Power

Hatha Yoga: The Hidden Language

The Divine Light Invocation

Realities of the Dreaming Mind

Seeds of Light

Time to be Holy

Glimpses of a Mystical Affair

From the Mating Dance to the Cosmic Dance

The Rose Ceremony

Radha, Diary of a Woman's Search (book and audio book)

In the Company of the Wise (book and audio book)

Radha's Story (video)

Can You Listen to a Woman

A Man's Journey to the Heart

DAVID FORSEE
(SWAMI GOPALANANDA)

TIMELESS BOOKS
PO Box 3543
Spokane, WA 99220-3543
1-800-251-9273
http://www.timeless.org
In Canada: Timeless Books, Box 9, Kootenay Bay, BC V0B 1X0
1-800-661-8711

2nd printing, May 1999

Printed in Canada

Editor: Karin Lenman
Cover and interior design by Warren Clark

Library of Congress Cataloging-in-Publication Data
    Forsee, David 1944–
    Can you listen to a woman:
    a man's journey to the heart / David Forsee
    (Swami Gopalananda).
        p.   cm.
    ISBN 0-931454-93-X (pbk: alk. paper)
    1. Forsee, David, 1944–. 2. Radha, Swami Sivananda, 1911–
    1995. 3. Spiritual biography—United States. 4. Femininity—
    Religious aspects. 5. Hindus—United States—Biography. I. Title
BL1175.F67A34   1999
294.5'092—dc21
{B}   98-50804
                                                        CIP

Published by

Timeless Books
Since 1978

Dedicated to my Spiritual Mother,
Swami Sivananda Radha,
who courageously challenged me
to recognize my own Radha nature.
This book is my offering to her
that she might know
in some small measure
her efforts were not in vain.

Contents

Acknowledgments

I am deeply indebted to my guru, Swami Sivananda Radha, who showed me a way through the "Maze" back to my spiritual home, and also to her guru, Swami Sivananda of Rishikesh, who had the courage to initiate a Western woman into the sacred order of sanyas. I also want to express my gratitude to Swami Radhananda, President of Yasodhara Ashram, for her steadfast encouragement and support of my efforts to write this book. Many times her diamond-like clarity helped me to keep on track with this work. Her direction never failed me.

Many people contributed to this project out of a sincere desire to further Swami Radha's work. Your encouragement and feedback helped me to take the next step and I am grateful for your help.

A special thanks goes to each of you who donated very generously to the production costs by purchasing a chapter of the book prior to its publication. Indirectly, your contribution also helped the Ashram's youth program. All proceeds from the sale of this book will go to supporting the program, which is dedicated to helping young people bring purpose and direction into their lives in very practical ways.

Finally, I wish to thank Donna (Swami Radhakrishnananda) and Alicia, who play such a large part in this story. Without them I would not have had a starting place in this path of love that led me to Swami Radha.

Swami Gopalananda
Yasodhara Ashram

Sometimes we are unaware that we are walking in God's Light. Sometimes it looks very dark. But after many long, dark, winter days, the first spring day comes with its first spring flowers and we think a miracle has happened. It was a very glorious day in my life when I met my guru, Swami Sivananda. After years of searching in the dark suddenly many things began to come to life. And yet without the darkness perhaps I would never have appreciated the Light.

~

Swami Radha

Introduction

Swami Radha's teachings invoke the feminine, the return to the goddess or Divine Mother. They are based on the feminine power of the Kundalini system as the path to Higher Consciousness. Life itself is the path. We are encouraged to reflect on our lives and actions to understand ourselves. As we do, the path keeps opening up before us. The teachings are secret, not because they are hidden in secret texts, but because they are so embedded in ordinary events. Many people are so busy anticipating the "big experience" that they miss the extraordinary in the ordinary, and it is in ordinary things that the teachings are brought to life.

In David Forsee's book, *Can You Listen to a Woman,* we meet a man who has lived a regular North American life, then made a commitment to the path of Swami Radha's teachings. Because of this commitment, his attachments to concepts of family life, work, and what it means to be a man had to be turned around or transformed. We see both his struggles and his determination to enter a new place in his mind. His story is personal—the story of a man who is willing to become intimate with the teachings, with the teacher—who is a woman—and ultimately with himself. *Can You Listen to a Woman* introduces us to a man who is willing to change, to come from his heart. His journey into the unknown is expressed in his willingness to reflect on his life, to penetrate the meaning of its events, and to act on this new understanding.

His story reflects the process of spiritual evolution. We see him go from David Forsee to Swami Gopalananda. When he made the commitment, he had to encounter the fierceness of reaction to changing an old way of life. In such times and mental states, it takes courage to ask for help, to turn to someone who has the wisdom of experience. Strength can be developed through gratitude for life and its challenges, and for the teacher's help and patience. Then the challenge, the teacher, the teachings, the Light, the gratitude, all become intertwined.

A commitment to spiritual life will continue to demand personal work. It is an ongoing path. There is refuge in the teachings, in the teacher, and in our own victories—in how we overcome the demons and dragons in our own lives.

Swami Radha told her disciples over and over that the way to understand the teachings is to write about their experience with her, and to read her autobiography[*] to see how the teachings came to life in her.

"Wisdom is a living thing," she said.

The path is open to anyone courageous enough to enter in, to be challenged and to take responsibility. Each one of us has a unique path and the power of reflection that can open it up for us. *Can You Listen to a Woman* shows us one man living his path.

Swami Radhananda
President, Yasodhara Ashram Society

---

[*] Swami Sivananda Radha, *Radha, Diary of a Woman's Search* (Spokane: Timeless Books, 1990).

CHAPTER ONE

Assignment

Soon after I moved to Yasodhara Ashram, Swami Radha gave me a ballpoint pen that had a little digital calendar built into its cap. I saw the gift as a nice gesture, but the thought that I was meant to write something with it never occurred to me. Instead, like a child temporarily enchanted with a new toy, I directed my efforts towards the ultimately fruitless task of trying to make the calendar work. I tried two or three times then gave up and put the pen into the top drawer of my desk where I promptly forgot it.

A year and a half later on a warm Sunday night in the middle of summer, Swami Radha spoke at satsang* and the last words of her talk that evening were, "…and I remember giving a pen to someone once and I'm still waiting to see if that pen is going to produce anything." I remember the humor and warmth in her voice when she said these words, but the message sailed directly across the room and embedded itself right where it was meant to. Immediately after satsang I rushed home, yanked open the top drawer of my desk, and with considerable relief found the pen still where I had left it. But the problem of what I was meant to do with the pen had remained in the drawer, as well. I still didn't have the story to go with it. In time the pen disappeared altogether and she never referred to it again.

---

* A spiritual service held each evening in yoga communities. The word means "company of the wise."

Tonight in Spokane, many years later, she sits across from me at her desk, hunched over, peering intently through a magnifying glass as she turns the pages of a miniature diary given to her in India by her guru, Swami Sivananda. We are reviewing the biography work so far. A soft, late night quiet fills the room. Outside, a street lamp casts its silvery glow onto the sheer curtains covering the window beside the desk. The lamplight gathers around her like a gentle, luminescent shawl. I can just make out the writing on the cover of the little diary as she holds it up to the light.

Compliments
of
J. Singh
Accountants
Bombay/Calcutta
1954

I sit watching her closely as she peers silently through the magnifying glass, sifting the returning memories. Thirty-two pages of tiny, indelible, single-syllable reminders of her six months with Gurudev, each page divided into an orderly alignment of consecutive days. I think of the incredible wealth, daily bread, carefully preserved in the form of a few key words. At all costs, her memory of this extraordinary place and time must be reliable.

As I look at her, I begin to feel waves of admiration and gratitude for the tremendous respect she brings to her life, here in this moment, and in all the moments past. She puts down the magnifying glass and looks up.

"If you do this biography work, it could bring about a lot of change in you. Can you see that?"

"Yes, I can."

"So now you understand why you can write about me only from your own experience?"

"I do."

"Go back to your diaries. Highlight the things that stand out for you now. Find out what is there. See how far you have come. You must be able to see how far you have come. Om Om."

~

Once when Swami Radha was describing her own early career as a writer, she showed me a photograph* taken when she was nineteen years old. The ethereal beauty of the young woman in the photograph took my breath away. Her clear, penetrating dark eyes looked straight into mine as if I, a stranger, had just addressed her by name. Swami Radha noticed, and a few days later presented me with the photograph.

That night was one of those special times when she would go back to the earliest memories of her growing-up years. These stories often affected me so deeply that the feelings could be almost overwhelming. Even now, I don't know why that period of her life was so important to me. So intimate and familiar were these stories that it was easy to become part of them, a silent observer sitting at the next table or walking along the same Berlin street.

She was just nineteen when the Berlin business paper, *Nachtaus Gabawas,* began publishing her short stories under the pen name "Lorenz". The editor called her regularly, knowing that she could always have a story ready for the next evening edition.

"Nicholas would call me up and say, 'You'd better come down here, the story is too long. You'll have to remove four lines.'"

Swami Radha laughed, remembering the phone calls that could come at any hour of the day or night.

"So I would go down to the building where they did the typesetting and printing, and I'd sit with the typesetter at this huge machine while he shifted the hot lead up to where I could take enough out to make

---

Cover photograph–Swami Radha at age nineteen.

the story fit the page. Afterwards, Nicholas and I would go over to Romanche's, which in those days was a popular café for writers and artists on Kurfurstendahm, and over coffee or a glass of wine, we would develop some ideas for my next assignment."

She chuckled again, recalling how Nicholas always phrased his question to her in the same way.

"Now then," he'd say, as he rummaged through the stuffed cardboard folders in his briefcase, "what is your next assignment?"

From there they would go into whatever ideas or thoughts came to mind.

One rainy night when she was walking home from one of their sessions, his question returned to her, only this time from a very different perspective.

"What is my assignment?" she asked herself as she walked along the dark, wet street.

Maybe there was a purpose to life after all, a particular job to do in this lifetime. If so, she wondered, what could it possibly be? There was no immediate answer, of course, and she put the question aside. It would come back to her many times in the tumultuous, tragic years ahead.

What is the purpose of life, and how much living does it take to get to the point where it is the only real question left to ask? Swami Radha had her own ways of encouraging her students to find the answer for themselves. But we had to be open and receptive and listening to get the message, which meant that a certain amount of mental/emotional self-control was necessary in order to hear it. Now, years later as I sit with Swami Radha late at night in her apartment in Spokane, her story about Nicholas and the assignment conjures up the memory of that ballpoint pen with the digital calendar built into its cap. Finally I understand.

CHAPTER TWO

Opening the Seal

In the summer of 1978 my wife and six-year-old daughter went for six weeks to Swami Radha's ashram on the shores of Kootenay Lake in British Columbia. The ashram and its yoga on the other side of the country, far from our home in northwestern Ontario, was of little interest to me at the time. I was happy to stay home and for a little while, anyway, to be on my own again, temporarily free of family obligations.

Happy, but not entirely free. It occurred to me after she'd been gone for a week that my wife's interest in these strange new pursuits could lead to changes in our marriage, perhaps dramatic changes, over which I had little control. With over a month to go before her planned return, I steeled myself against further worry and buried myself in lots of overtime work in the bush. Relief from the stifling heat of those long summer days came only at night when I hauled pulpwood along the cool north-shore highway of Lake Superior into Thunder Bay. One night, a full moon crossed the lake and followed me all the way home, casting its silvery light on the highway ahead. Before long the loneliness that had been with me all day vanished like a forgotten dream.

At the end of August Donna and Alicia came home from the ashram. They were very excited.

"It is a wonderful place," Donna said.

"That's good," I responded, happy to see them both again, looking very much as I had known them before they left. Our time apart had filled my heart with renewed appreciation for the wonderful blessings of family life.

"It's really wonderful," she continued. "You'd love it there, too."

Ah. Not likely. The idea was not at all appealing to me. I had never felt comfortable in groups, I was not a joiner and had never been happy in the company of people who were.

My stand was on firm ground and I said to my wife with some confidence, "No. I don't think I would love it at all."

To my surprise she didn't rise to the challenge. Something had changed. In the past this would have been good for a little jostling of wills. But not this time. In fact, she never raised the issue again.

A few months later, Donna and a friend got together enough people to bring someone from the ashram to present a workshop called Life Seals®. My own lack of interest in yoga had done little to dampen her enthusiasm, and she happily warmed to the subject whenever she encountered anyone who appeared to be interested. Quite a number must have been because in only a few days more than a dozen people signed up, an extraordinary response considering the small, normally conservative population of our isolated, northern Ontario bush town. In spite of the enthusiasm around me, though, I continued to doubt that the workshop could hold much for me that would be worthwhile.

Many years later when I was telling Swami Radha about my initial resistance to the workshop, she remarked that the Life Seals process removes a burden from our conscience which, in turn, starts to free the soul.

"It is the ego that resists what the Higher Self already knows," she said.

That rang true for me. Even making the drawings for the seal was like opening a door into a long-forgotten room and seeing something very precious in the light now pouring into the center of the room. The swami leading our workshop had said, "Your Life Seals can stay with you for many years. Now and again, your mind will return to the drawings, the seals, as if seeing them for the first time, and a whole new level of interpretation and understanding will come to you." That, too, has been my experience.

Like most people going into the Life Seals for the first time, I knew nothing of how the process worked. My response to the instructions given to us the first night—to make crayon drawings representing our senses, our likes and dislikes, plus various other aspects of ourselves including the mind and something called the essence—was apprehension and doubt along with a healthy dose of fear as well. Twenty-seven drawings in all. I seriously questioned if it was even humanly possible to make twenty-seven drawings before sunrise the next morning. On the other hand, I was curious to see how my unconscious mind would represent aspects of myself that I had never thought about in the past.

Quality in work, one of my personal likes, appeared in a drawing of my old car. The language I used to describe the car—steady, solid, faithful after many years and miles—and the feelings behind the words soon made it apparent that I was describing something far beyond the car itself. These were qualities that I valued in myself. Another drawing of a figure sitting alone at a dining table stirred old memories of many meals eaten alone during my adolescence. When I say "stirred" I mean anger stirring as I again felt the humiliation and isolation from those times.

I began to understand that mind was far more than a generator of concepts and powerful emotions. Again I looked at the seal and this time understood that all the drawings had the same potential to release their hidden secrets. My eyes went to the hands in the upper left corner representing my sense of touch. They had seemed so important when I traced them from my own hands, but now they seemed more like the hands of a stranger. I stood gazing at the drawing for a long time not saying anything. Finally the workshop leader asked me how I used my sense of touch.

Without turning to look at him I said, "I love the feel of machine tools, well made, beautifully crafted. They seem to soften with oil and use." Long pause. "Touch can also reassure someone, or show support and encouragement to another."

"Who, for instance?"

"Well, it wouldn't have to be anyone in particular. Just where I sensed that a young person might need some reassurance that he's doing okay."

"A young person?"

"Yes." But my voice was barely audible behind the tears locked in my throat and chest.

"Whose hands are they?"

"My father's. But he never treated me that way. Never."

The sorrow seemed to come up from a deep place in the distant past. My father had been dead for years, but from my response it was obvious that he occupied a living space in my mind. Now here he was offering his hands to me for the first time. How could I refuse? For years I had watched those hands gripping a hammer, pushing a snow shovel, fixing things, steering the car. I reached my father through his hands, and I learned from him and loved him, but he was so remote that it was impossible for me to tell him so. It all came out through this simple little drawing—tracing really—of a pair of hands. My hands, my father's hands—who could tell?—they were so much alike.

The challenge for me coming out of this seal was to find out how much my experience growing up had influenced my ability to express love to a child. I thought about Alicia. Was there a way that I could teach my daughter about life that would appeal to her intelligence while allowing her to keep her integrity and dignity intact? That night I wrote in my diary:

> Criticize and you teach criticism.
> Judge and you diminish self-worth.
> Withhold praise and you affirm lack of self-confidence.
> Condemn and you teach shame.
>
> Humor brings laughter.
> Friendship teaches forgiveness.
> Encouragement gives hope.
> Affection builds trust.
> Acceptance is love.

CHAPTER THREE

Journey

The summer following the Life Seals workshop, I went to the ashram to take an introductory course in yoga. I went more out of curiosity than from any longing to study yoga. It never crossed my mind that I would get to meet Swami Radha—yet on my way to lunch the first day of the course I did meet her. She stood at the entrance to the dining room, smiling and nodding to people as they went by, warmly inviting as I walked towards her. She looked radiant in the noonday sun despite the arthritis that was constantly with her and which a few years earlier had almost killed her. She was sixty-nine years old.

I remember being struck by her physical size as I drew closer to her. She appeared taller than I had expected, certainly tall enough for the two of us to face each other at eye level. However, my sense of sight was playing tricks. Swami Radha was actually quite tiny, just over five feet, and since I am well over six feet the likelihood of us being able to face each other at eye level simply didn't exist, at least in the physical sense. Today, I think it is more likely that a part of my mind recognized her for who she was. Something told me she was a spiritual teacher of great substance and depth, and in that recognition I felt an immediate trust. That surprised me. It was not my usual way of entering into anything new and different. Oddly, Swami Radha seemed delighted to see me, as if we were old friends encountering each other again after a long absence.

It was in the midst of these first impressions that Alicia, my wife's daughter from a previous relationship, ran by.

"Hi, Daddy!" she called out as she raced into Main House for lunch.

Swami Radha watched after her for a moment and then turned and looked at me.

"She calls you Daddy?"

I nodded and smiled.

"Hm."

Swami Radha looked at me intently, her expression thoughtful and kind. Having previously met Donna and Alicia, she knew something of the circumstances that had brought us together as a family.

"It's not so often that a man can accept another man's child," she said.

Her remark surprised me but it helped to explain some of the confusion around my initial responses to Alicia.

"Well, it's true I was reluctant at first," I said. "I just didn't have any idea if I could make the kind of commitment that the word 'daddy' implied."

That was the real reason. What I had told Alicia soon after the three of us had decided to live together was that I didn't want to cause confusion in her relationship with her biological father. That was true but hardly relevant since he had left the family soon after she was born. With Swami Radha's question, my mind went back over the play of circumstances that had led me to act decisively and make a commitment to Alicia.

"We worked it out," I told Swami Radha, "and we seem to be doing well together."

Swami Radha nodded. She seemed happy to hear about my family. But as I was to learn in time, her interest in my relationship with Alicia had its roots in the distant past of her own childhood in Europe. She had been very close to her father, in fact thought of him as her best friend during her growing-up years. Her inquiry had come from the perspective of her own experience, which made it easy for me to respond, and because she had spoken to a part of my life that was very dear to me, I naturally responded warmly towards her.

Half an hour after lunch that day, I bounded up the steps leading to the ashram's guest lodge with an energy I hadn't felt for years. At the top of the steps I suddenly ran into a wall of Light. It flashed across my eyes like sheet lightning across a prairie sky. I stopped and looked around to see where it had come from. There was no one else close by, the afternoon was warm and sunny, and the sky was clear blue. Yet there was no question that something startling had just happened. I felt light and happy and filled with goodwill, so different from the judgmental and critical mood I had taken into class that morning. Now it was as if I had left that part of my mind at the bottom of the hill and something else was pouring in to fill the space.

"People here are trying to live according to their Ideals. Men and women here are trying to live a spiritual life," I exclaimed. "I cannot believe that such a place as this exists in the world. I am so happy to be here."

And with that the veil closed. But I was no longer the same person. I could no longer sustain the belief that I was separate from other people.

It would be easy to write my new convictions off to a youthful idealism, a temporary lapse in perspective. But it would be more precise to say that my experience resulted from a momentary suspension of criticism which allowed a fleeting glimpse into another dimension. Somewhere between the dining room and the steps to the guest lodge my intellectual guard stumbled and wisdom seized the moment. In an instant it was gone, but I held onto the experience—the insights—that had spun me around a hundred and eighty degrees. The Light was so powerful and freeing that I never forgot it, even in the midst of crushing self-doubt that descended out of the darkness years later.

After supper that evening Swami Radha invited the people taking the course over to her house for a visit. As I walked along the road to Many Mansions, it occurred to me that I knew almost nothing about her and even less about yoga. Yet that didn't seem to be making much difference. I was happy to be in her ashram studying the yoga she was offering, and it seemed the opening created by that sense of happiness and well-being was allowing Swami Radha into my life. Without my realizing it a fundamental shift in attitude had come over me like a wave of light, bringing with it a purpose for living and a commitment that has been central to my life ever since.

~

On a sunny Tuesday morning in fall, a little over a year after our first meeting, Swami Radha and I turned onto the Don Valley Parkway in Toronto and headed north out of the city. Beside us the southbound lanes were choked with rush hour traffic crawling towards the down-town core.

"This is an automatic?" she asked, as I accelerated into the passing lane.

The car was just a few months old, a metallic-brown Accord with tan velour upholstery. It was the first new car I had owned in years.

"Yes. I've driven a standard for years, but I like this. It's a nice change."

Swami Radha was quiet for a moment. I thought she was just making polite conversation, her way of settling into our trip. But I was wrong. She was thinking about something quite specific.

"A few years ago, the husband of one of my students in California offered to drive me out to the airport when I was leaving to come back to the ashram. I accepted, of course. His car wasn't automatic. He seemed to be shifting gears all the time, never taking his hand off the lever, and the way he zoomed in and out of the traffic made me wonder: Does driving like that have anything to do with power and being a man? What you have here seems much better."

We were about eight minutes into our three-day trip and already I could see another dimension of our journey starting to open up—one that would challenge many of my most cherished concepts and beliefs about being male. My mind went back to the oriental carpet dealer Swami Radha and I had visited the previous week. We had gone to his warehouse on Eglinton Avenue looking for information about a carpet that had been given to her many years ago. When we arrived Swami Radha showed him a color photograph of the carpet so that he would have more than just a verbal description to refer to. He reacted as if we'd just presented him with a dead fish.

"What am I supposed to do with this?" he demanded. "I can't tell anything from this. Could be anything."

His abrupt tone of voice surprised me but it did not appear to affect Swami Radha. Her voice was steady and patient as she again asked him to look at the picture. Could he see anything that might give her some indication of how old the carpet might be and what it could be worth? He looked at her for a moment without saying anything, then picked up a magnifying glass and peered through it at the photograph. After a minute or two of concentrated silence he made a few perfunctory observations, then handed the photograph back to her signifying the end of our interview.

Out on the street I could no longer restrain myself.

"How could he treat you that way?" I said. "I can't believe anyone would be so rude to you!"

Swami Radha laughed. "But, David," she said. "I didn't go to him to be flattered. I went to get information about a carpet that had been given to me and I found out what I needed. Why would I want anything else from him?"

Why indeed. Why would anyone who had achieved emotional independence want anything from anyone? I could accept the logic of the question easily enough, but at the same time I felt uneasy. Where would I fit into the life of someone who didn't need me? Why would I even want to try?

Ahead of us the office towers and high-rise condominiums of North York stood in stark relief against a clear blue sky. Swami Radha and I were on our way to Sioux Lookout, nineteen hundred kilometers to the northwest—just the two of us traveling together for three days, perhaps longer. All the previous week, almost from the moment she had proposed the trip, I had been anxious, then excited, then anxious again, not knowing why she wanted to come with me, or what it would lead to. At one point I had even called one of her close disciples in the ashram to find out what I should do about our accommodation.

"Where should I stay?" I asked him. "Does she need a room of her own? Is it right for us to stay in the same room even though she's almost twice my age?"

I don't think it was too hard for the swami to hear the anxiety in my voice.

"She's great fun to travel with," he said, ignoring my questions. "The best thing you can do is just sit back and relax and enjoy the trip. Just be your normal self. That's the best thing you can do for her."

I wasn't so sure that my "normal" self would be the best thing at all, but now that we were actually together and in motion my anxiety floated away unnoticed. I was happy just to be sitting beside her, moving with her, accepting the gift of this remarkable opportunity.

Swami Radha often referred to what she called her Divine Committee, a kind of mystical management group responsible for making sure that her evolution took the correct course. She used to say that as a sanyasin* it wouldn't matter much what she thought about how her life should be or what she might have preferred if her Divine Committee had other plans. As a sanyasin, her job was to listen, observe, and obey. She was very tuned in to her Divine Committee, and perhaps to mine, too. Something would happen—our road trip was a good example— and she would grow thoughtful, her eyes focusing off somewhere, and she would say, "Well, I wonder what my Divine Committee is up to now?" or "I wonder what my Divine Committee has in store for me?" Then she would wait for the answer. Sometimes it came quickly, other times not.

---

* A renunciate.

"You cannot command the Divine," she would often remind those of us who had a tendency towards impatience.

Often I had yearned for a similar connection in my own life, though hardly with the same degree of consistency or trust. Ambition tempered my desire for the Divine in shades of ambiguity, and I would go for long periods of time without a passing reflective thought. Then something would happen to challenge my indifference, sometimes a dramatic event, other times nothing more than a subtle, sweet pause urging me to question what I was doing with my life. Such moments were rare.

There was no doubt in Swami Radha's mind that our Divine Committees had somehow collaborated to create this opportunity for us to travel together. Although it would take several years for me to understand the larger meaning of this singular event, as a journey of inception its symbolic meaning was not lost on me even then. I would never have used the term "guru-disciple relationship" at the time, but it was evident that something unusual and special was starting to unfold, and that I was being invited to enter it.

It had all started when I phoned her just a few hours after arriving in Toronto on personal business.

Swami Radha was in the city to do some workshops, and when she heard that I was going to be there at the same time, she encouraged me to call her if I had time.

"Come over," she said. "We can have lunch together."

"Yes. It'll take me about thirty minutes to cross town but I'll leave right away. And thank you!"

Just hearing her voice lifted my spirits.

Traffic was unusually light that morning and I made it across town easily. Over lunch I told her that I needed to be in the city for about a week and that I would be starting the drive back to Sioux Lookout, the northwestern Ontario town where I lived, about a day after her last workshop in Toronto. Swami Radha was scheduled to fly from Toronto to Thunder Bay where she planned to visit a student of hers who was seriously ill with cancer. After that, she was going to travel on to Sioux Lookout to present a Music and Consciousness workshop to our yoga group. Everything appeared to be in place and working out perfectly. Swami Radha nodded to herself.

"Maybe we could drive together from here to Sioux Lookout. What would you say to that?" she asked.

"Well, um, we could," I said, trying to accommodate this sudden shift in my well-ordered plans.

Inside, my head started to spin. She's so refined. Why on earth would she want to spend three days with me? It's such a long trip by car. Wouldn't she get bored with mile after mile of nothing but trees to look at?

"I would be delighted to have you come with me," I said.

"Great! Then that's what we'll do. That's just great."

And that's how it started. She seemed genuinely happy at the prospect.

It was near dusk of our first day on the road by the time we turned into the parking lot of the Ramada Inn, just where the Trans-Canada Highway enters Sault Ste. Marie. The setting sun cast a fiery glow across the dark-tinted glass and brick entrance to the hotel lobby. I was tired and happy to be stopping. We had driven almost five hundred miles our first day.

Our room on the second floor looked out over the parking lot to an A&W drive-in, a doughnut shop, and a GM dealership across the high-way from the motel. Their glaring neon signs commanded all the powers of my concentration as I stood staring out the window of our room praying that what I had heard when we came into the room wasn't—couldn't be—what I knew it was. It just couldn't be. But there was no mistaking the sounds of sex as a crescendo of creaking and groaning poured through the thin wall from the room next door. I continued to stare out the window as the first prickly flush of perspiration started on my forehead and under my arms. Why now? I thought. Why now of all times? At the intersection the traffic light changed. A huge tractor-trailer slowly turned onto the Trans-Canada and headed west, its twin stacks blowing black diesel into the cold night air. I didn't have to turn around to know that Swami Radha was standing behind me waiting for me to put the bags down. She must have heard it, too. Or maybe not. How would I know? What should I say? Do I just pretend it isn't happening?

"Doesn't sound like *that* much fun," she said softly from behind.

I turned and stared at her. Her face was serious, but so open and kind that I started to chuckle with relief.

"I'll get the rest of our luggage," I said, and excused myself.

Outside in the hall I quickly lit up a smoke, inhaled deeply, and waited for the calming effect to take hold. I could never have imagined it was going to be like this, I thought, as I stood waiting in front of the dull green elevator doors. What is it about her? Everything seems to grow larger than life around her. Is this what it's like to be in the Light, swirling round and round in a sea of confusion? That's what it felt like: round and round like a vortex, alarming and exhilarating at the same time with all the spontaneity of a fascinating dream, and never knowing what was going to happen next.

After two weeks in the city I had already forgotten how crisp and clear the northern nights could be in the fall. I glanced up at the stars as I walked across the parking lot to the car. There were so many to see at once, as if all the stars in the universe had gathered around this one spot just to be with us for the night. I gathered up the rest of our luggage along with a windbreaker and an old blue sweater I always kept with me on the road, locked the car, and hurried back across the parking lot towards the hotel lobby.

CHAPTER FOUR

Purpose

That night over supper in the hotel dining room we took the next steps towards deepening our friendship. Swami Radha began by telling me something of her life in Europe before she emigrated to Canada, long before India and her initiation into sanyas. I was glad she wanted to talk. After a full day of driving capped by the disconcerting circumstances greeting our arrival at the inn, I didn't think I had a lot left over for anything more than polite conversation. Perhaps she sensed the tension in me because her voice and demeanor exuded the kind of calmness I had experienced in the past from people who are confident enough to accept others without judgment. Her acceptance of me was important. The more I felt it the more relaxed I became.

From her earliest memories Swami Radha recalled an affection and ease with her father that would have been more typical of an intimate, long-standing adult friendship than a relationship between parent and child. She laughed as she told the story of a business associate of her father visiting the family home one day when she was about four years old. The man was shocked when the little girl came into the room and addressed her father by his first name. In those days it was unheard of for a child to assume such familiarity with a parent.

"He said to my father, 'Why do you allow this?' and it put my father on the spot, you see, because he had never questioned it. My father thought for a moment, then turned to me for the answer.

" 'It's very simple,' I said. 'You call your best friend by his first name, and you are my best friend, so I call you by your first name.' "

Swami Radha laughed again, as if it had all just happened yesterday instead of almost seventy years ago. Yet the way she told the story made it as immediate for me as if it were yesterday. I had a sense of what that kind of friendship could be like between a father and daughter, and the story, simple as it was, touched me deeply.

Her relationship with her mother, on the other hand, was never pleasant. Swami Radha described her mother as a very worldly woman, gorgeous, a kind of Marilyn Monroe with dark red hair. She said that her mother could walk down a street in any city and men would invariably turn to gaze after her, yet none of them would have guessed that this apparently self-assured woman spent most of her days caught in the grip of terrible jealousy and fear. Her mother was so consumed by these powerful emotions that she tried to abort her only child in the early stages of pregnancy.

"My parents divorced when I was eleven years old," Swami Radha told me after the waiter had come to take our order, "and in all the confusion around their separation, I was sent by mistake to a boys' boarding school. When I arrived at the school it was too late in the day to be sent back. The headmaster and his wife gave me their daughter's room while they tried to sort out the mistake.

"By the next morning I had decided that I wanted to stay at the school. My family must have worked it out with the school because I ended up staying until I graduated six years later. That was a very good time in my life. Living with the boys taught me how to stand on my own feet and look after myself and by the time I graduated I knew what it meant to be able to do that."

She sat quietly for a moment, seemingly absorbed by the memories of that time. In fact, she was thinking of something else, a favorite uncle whose marriage to an older woman had caused considerable upset in her family.

"My uncle's new wife was at least fifteen years older than he was although I was too young to notice, or at least it didn't strike me as odd. And I liked them both, so it puzzled me that their marriage caused such a fuss in our household. Then I visited my uncle's house one day—I was only four or five years old at the time—and quite by accident, I discovered that there was something very different about their marriage. I happened to be upstairs by myself when I noticed that the door to my uncle's room, which was usually closed, had been left open. Being naturally curious, I went to the door and peeked in and there sitting on an altar at the front of the room was a magnificent golden Buddha. I was astonished! Why did my uncle have this in his room? Later my father told me that they were practicing Buddhists. It turned out that my uncle was her disciple and they had married in order to deflect unnecessary attention and criticism."

The story of Swami Radha's uncle got me thinking about friendship between men and women and if it is even possible. In the early years of our marriage my wife and I had placed a great deal of value on our friendship, but now with some of the emotional fires from those early years abated, it was hard to see clearly what the purpose of our marriage might be. Beyond the practical needs of sustaining a family, I didn't know.

By the time we finished dessert, most of the supper crowd had come and gone and the room had grown quiet. Over coffee Swami Radha started to tell me the story of Wolfgang, her husband. Of all she said that night, it is the image of Wolfgang that remains most vivid in my memory, perhaps because I identified with him in some way or perhaps for some other reason that is still a mystery to me. I just know that the impact of Wolfgang's story has stayed with me ever since. When Swami Radha happened to show me a photograph of Wolfgang a few years ago, it startled me. For a moment I thought I recognized someone I once knew long ago.

Swami Radha laughed when she described their first encounter over the phone, and how she had agreed to see him even though they had never met.

"I had planned to spend time with some friends," she explained, "but they phoned just before coming over to say that a friend of theirs whom they hadn't seen in ages was visiting and would it be all right to bring him along, too. I said he could come if he wanted, and then I added jokingly, 'Just make sure he behaves correctly.' I didn't know it but by that time Wolfgang had the receiver in his hand. He said, 'I promise.' And that's how we started.

"Wolfgang had just been released from a concentration camp. Actually it was the second time for him. Each time, his mother paid off the Nazis and got him out—the first time cost her almost half a million marks; the second time much more—but that couldn't keep going on indefinitely. He was an aristocrat, you see—a baron, actually—and the Nazis were definitely against the aristocracy. During the First World War, Wolfgang had been on the Kaiser's staff and that made the Nazis even more suspicious. Even so, his title and the family wealth were some protection. But then the war started to turn against Hitler, and after that Wolfgang had no protection.

"From the beginning I challenged Wolfgang. He was born into an aristocratic family and had been trained as an officer in the military, but he had never really questioned his upbringing. One time he showed me on a map where the German army had invaded France in the First World War. I think it was called the Battle of the Marne. Anyway, he seemed quite proud of the fact that the victory had cost the lives of just twenty thousand German troops.

"I was horrified. 'Wolfgang!' I said. 'Twenty thousand young men, some barely eighteen years old, not even having lived a life yet, sacrificed for what? For what purpose? And to satisfy whose ambition?' He couldn't answer. He was just stunned by the questions but eventually he began to see things differently. In time he became very generous and helped me to get visas for Jewish friends so they could get out of the country. That was at a time when helping the Jews was considered treason."

Swami Radha picked up a spoon and turned it slowly in the candlelight. Together we watched the play of soft light on its smooth, curving surface.

"It was only about a year and a half before Wolfgang was once again picked up by the Gestapo. This time there was no getting away. He was tried in court and found guilty of treason. After the trial he was sent to a concentration camp near the Dutch border, where he was held before being transferred to Buchenwald. That's where his mother and I saw him for the last time," she said, carefully placing down the spoon. "When we went to visit him, the officer in charge greeted me with a hand kiss and then had tea and pastries brought in on a silver service. The Nazis were against the aristocracy, but when it served their purpose, they were quite willing to use the hated aristocracy's ways for their own ends.

"After this we were shown into a room reserved for political prisoners. Men with swollen bellies and knees sat on the floor along the walls. My mother-in-law said, 'But Wolfgang isn't here.'

" 'You just don't recognize him,' I said, and I pointed to one of the men sitting on the floor against the wall. When she saw her son she broke down. He was just bone covered with skin. All his joints were full of water and his stomach was bloated. When I knelt down to speak to him, right away he asked me about the baby. I was pregnant, you see, when Wolfgang was arrested. But under the strain of the trial and being hounded by the Gestapo after he was imprisoned, I had a miscarriage and lost the baby.

"A week after this visit I received an anonymous telephone call from a woman who said, 'You will be given notification in two weeks that your husband has died of heart failure, but that won't be true. He will have been killed. I can't give you my name or any more information than that,' and she hung up. Two weeks later, the notification arrived in the mail."

She paused, looked closely at me, then took up her story.

"You see, the tragedy was that I could have spared him the pain had I understood what real love is. After Wolfgang's last court appearance before he was sent to the concentration camp, his lawyer came to see me with Wolfgang's briefcase. The lawyer said, 'I have arranged for the two of you to have an interview without any witnesses—police or otherwise. In the briefcase is a gun with five bullets. Give it to him. Don't let him go to a concentration camp. It's terrible.'

"But like most Germans I didn't know what the concentration camps were. When I had my interview with Wolfgang, I just didn't have the nerve to give it to him. My argument was, 'I love my husband. I love my husband. Surely he will be all right and I will see him again.' So I couldn't give him the gun. I made several attempts but I just couldn't do it. He seemed not to notice or maybe he thought I was nervous and tense, I don't know. I don't know what was going through his mind.

"In any case, I didn't do it and a couple of months later it was all over. It was only then I realized that if I had given him the gun, that would have been love. But I was thinking, I love my husband. I can't do this to him."

Swami Radha looked almost translucent in the soft candlelight as she paused for a sip of water. I tried to imagine what it must have been like for her to have carried the burden of such a terrible solution in her own hands as she sat for the last time within reach of the man she had loved and married. I could not imagine doing anything different from what she had done, yet I knew she was right about love. At the same time the anguish on her face revealed the pain that was still alive in her memory. But there was something else, too. She was angry.

"You see, David, it didn't have to happen," she said, looking at me intently. "I told him not to go that morning. I said, 'Wolfgang, the police will be at the house. Don't go.' Did he listen to me? No. He said, 'Don't be silly. Why do you worry your head about me? I'll be all right.'

"But I knew. Twice before the Gestapo had taken him in for questioning and each time his mother paid someone to have him released. But how often were they going to be willing to do that? Wolfgang left the apartment that morning and when he arrived at the house where the documents were made, the Gestapo were waiting for him. That's what happened."

She paused, but kept looking straight at me.

"What is it with men?" she asked. "Do they think women don't have any intelligence…that women have nothing intelligent to say? Is that why they don't listen?"

Her question stood. I had nothing to say. She took another sip of water, then looked away.

During supper a north wind had chilled the night air almost to freezing. Either that or the story of Wolfgang continued to affect me. I couldn't stop shivering as we walked together around the perimeter sidewalk of the parking lot. Swami Radha was not one to linger over sad memories, though. She was excited and full of energy and had already turned her mind to something else, although the wind and the traffic noise made it hard to hear. It may be that I was just tired from the day's traveling, but I could scarcely follow what she was saying. Besides, from the few words I did pick up, it seemed to me that she was talking about something far too important to be communicated in a wind storm. I wanted her to wait until we got back to our room where at least it would be quiet and warm. It never occurred to me that according to the Divine Will, the conditions were probably just right for the message she was trying to convey.

"Something took birth," she said, "and you can call it consciousness or energy, or even the soul, but then you would have to clarify what you mean by that. If I use myself as an example, once that consciousness or vortex of energy had taken form it was given the name 'Sylvia' by someone else. Sylvia started as a daughter and in time she became a dancer, a writer, a wife—but none of these things gave any lasting happiness. Then Sylvia went to India and Radha came into being. Now what? What about Sylvia?"

Swami Radha paused and looked at me to see if I was still with her. I was but just barely.

"I couldn't just get rid of Sylvia," she said, answering her own question. "I had to incorporate her in some way. Otherwise my mind would become dangerously split between the two. Sylvia had to learn to become the handmaiden to Radha. My life, with all that it had been up until the time of my initiation into sanyas, had now to be lifted up, transformed into a larger awareness. There had to be some purpose for the trials and the suffering that I had gone through, that everyone goes through in one way or another. That is what Swami Sivananda gave to me, David, a way to make sense of my life and to see its purpose."

Her ideas were new to me and difficult to follow. I had never thought about why I was here, why I had been given this life. I had just taken it for granted and assumed that it was up to me to make something of it, to find satisfaction in the work I did or in the relationships I formed. Now I was being challenged by a simple question I had never considered: What is the purpose of my life? In the context of all she had said over supper, all that had brought us together for this journey, the questions were starting to come to me. For what purpose had I been given this life and what did the circumstances of my birth—the family I was born into, the influences in my growing-up years—have to do with that purpose? Even starting to ask the questions left me feeling almost overwhelmed by the power behind them.

Birth, Sex, Love, Pain, Death—all coming together at a crossroads named after Mother Mary. I shivered with the realization of what was being presented to me and I felt a deep desire for sleep. Beside me Swami Radha was happy and excited and I wondered for a moment where she got the energy to keep going like this.

It was after eleven when I finally got into bed. Across the room, Swami Radha was sitting at the desk reading aloud from a manuscript "in progress." When it became apparent that I was fading quickly, she continued on her own in silence. I was just on the edge of sleep when she came over to my bed, leaned over and kissed me softly on the cheek.

"Have a good dream," she said, and got into the bed next to mine.

Then a very wonderful thing happened. In the silent darkness something touched me softly, first on my right cheek, then delicately across my forehead, and then it was gone into the night like a wisp carried on an evanescent breeze. I was startled and must have said something because Swami Radha responded in the darkness.

"Oh. Did you feel that?"

"Yes," I said, but I didn't dare ask what it was.

"Yes," she said. "That's it. Om Om, sleep well."

And I did.

CHAPTER FIVE

Choices

As you round a particular bend in the Trans-Canada Highway just west of Sault Ste. Marie, a magnificent view of Lake Superior suddenly appears before you, spreading out like a vast golden plain in the morning sun. It is almost impossible not to feel a little awe and wonder at the sight. Even on rainy, overcast days when the gray mist hangs suspended in the trees along the shoreline, the power and mystery of Lake Superior can still be felt. For tourists, hunters, wilderness buffs, and the people who live here, the North Shore, as the region around Lake Superior is called, is truly one of the natural wonders of the world.

However, for people traveling across the region by car it's a different story. Most of the celebrated beauty remains hidden behind an interminable band of coniferous forest crowding the highway all the way to the Manitoba border. After a few hours, this endless expanse of pine and spruce can get downright tedious. I know this. I have come home along this road many times and I know it almost too well.

Towards mid-afternoon on the second day of our trip, somewhere between White River and Marathon, Swami Radha put down the newsmagazine she had been reading aloud, paused to look out the window, then turned to me with a profoundly challenging question.

"Why would anyone want to live here?" she asked.

Why indeed? The same question had been put to me several years earlier by an Inuit woman in the eastern Arctic.

"What is it like there?" she had asked, after hearing that I was leaving Baffin Island to take up a new job at a CBC* station in Thunder Bay.

"Well," I said, "there's lots of trees and lakes and it's really beautiful, rugged country…" but already I could hear the tentativeness in my voice undermining my efforts to sound convincing.

"Doesn't sound so good," she said, shaking her head as she gazed across the bay at the hills on the other side.

"Why? What do you mean?"

"Can't see anything. All those trees. You can't see very far when there are so many trees. I don't think I would like that place."

The Inuit can be very practical when it comes to matters of what they like and don't like. Here was someone who had lived all her life on land where it takes a hundred years for a willow tree to reach its full stature of two and a half inches, on land where it is not unusual for a hunter to travel for several days over the ice floes and steep mountain passes before signs of migrating caribou start to appear. She knew that in a treeless terrain where the wind and snow can transform the land into an impenetrable sea of white in a matter of minutes, survival for herself and for the whole network of extended family that sustained her depended on being able to identify sources of food and protection long before they were needed. In a land as cold and hard as the Arctic tundra, survival is calculated in very practical terms. And yet it is this same land that gave me the gift of peace and acceptance to a degree that I had never before experienced in my life. I loved the Arctic. The only thing that could ever have taken me away from it was divine intervention.

It came one morning when the station manager in Thunder Bay, Ontario, called to offer me a job in news and current affairs. I said no, I wasn't ready to leave the Arctic yet. I needed more time. But that's not what he wanted to hear. Later the same day, Pat Reilly, the man who

---

* Canadian Broadcasting Corporation.

had given me my first job in public radio, called from Yellowknife and told me to think again.

"You've learned all you can in Frobisher Bay*," he said. "If you want to do more in public broadcasting you'll have to go to a place that can challenge you."

That night after supper I called Thunder Bay and accepted the job. Afterwards I walked down to the beach where the hunters stored their boats for the winter. In the gathering dusk the boats looked like a row of beached whales lying on their sides on the granite-colored sand. In a few weeks though, once breakup came, all that would change. The hunters would come and take their boats across the ice floes to the open water where the seals were to be found this time of year. When they returned, they would make sure that meat and skins were taken to the elderly first—a ritual that has helped to maintain the integrity of the people for thousands of years.

Already the sea ice was starting to soften into the shallow turquoise pools that appear every year as spring approaches. Each day the sun rose a little higher in the sky to push the winter darkness further to the north. The afternoon breezes, warmed ever so slightly by the sun, carried the pungent smell of the open sea into the village and filled the air with expectancy.

How many times had I crossed the frozen bay, coming home in the winter darkness at the end of a hunt, longing for warmth and the deep sleep that comes with exhaustion. And the day, almost exactly a year ago, when I took my snow machine onto the sea ice and drove as fast as I could down the bay, pounding over the hard, rough snow until the vibration up my spine got to be too much and I had to stop. Then, sitting alone in the vast white silence under a brilliant sun thinking, At any moment the power sustaining me could change its mind and I wouldn't last an hour. For the first time in my life I recognized a power

---

* Now called Iqaluit.

greater than my own ego, and the release that came with that recognition was magnificent.

But not this year. This year I would be two thousand miles to the southwest, returning to the mainstream of life. The thought filled me with an almost unbearable sorrow. I turned away from the silent beach and started to walk home. In the fading light it was hard to see the path leading back to the main road.

"It's not easy for me to answer your question, Swami Radha. If I hadn't left the Arctic to go to Thunder Bay, I never would have met Donna and Alicia, and it was through Donna that I eventually got to the ashram and met you. So I don't know. I don't know what the influences are that bring these things into play. I think I'm doing what I want to do in life, making my own choices and all that. But then completely unexpected things happen that in time become the real reason why I am doing anything. The North—both here and in the Arctic—is where I found the most happiness I have ever had in my life and mostly that had to do with friendship and living closely with other people, not with any particular ambition or career choice.

"The night before I left Frobisher Bay for the last time, I cried when I went to say good-bye to my friend Jonah and his family. They had been so accepting and decent. Jonah had taught me how to live on the land and we'd worked so well together. I felt deeply about leaving them, maybe knowing, on one level anyway, that I would probably never see them again. That was hard. For sure I've learned a lot of very practical skills in the North which has been good for me to do. But I've also experienced what I think is real love, too."

Swami Radha sat looking out the window at the road ahead, not saying anything. I was quiet, too. I had never understood so clearly that friendship had been such a large part of my connection to the North.

"Have you ever thought about unfinished business?" she asked.

"Unfinished business? Well...maybe...I don't know...."

"Or is it mainly the challenge? Challenges can be in many places, you know. If you had no restrictions whatsoever, what is it really that you would want to do?"

"You mean different from what I'm doing now? I don't think I would make any changes...maybe in how I do things...but not in what I'm doing. The first time I saw Donna's house in Sioux Lookout at the end of the road by the lake, I went down to the shore and sat on a rock and almost immediately I was hit with a very powerful feeling that this was an important place, a very important place. I don't know why I felt that way but I did. When I went up to the house, I said to her, 'You know, you really must keep this place. You must hang onto this place. It's really important here.' Then we went walking up the road and I just kept saying that to her. And, really, I hardly knew her at that time."

"Well," Swami Radha said, "you probably have some unfinished business. What it is I don't know. Perhaps something in a past life not finished. What I can see is...um...I'll put it this way. I know my unfinished business from a past life. Sometimes it has been very easy to see and sometimes it has not, that's just the way it is. But whenever I had a suspicion that something may have been unfinished business from a past life, I would always wait for additional confirmation. How do you find out? Dreams are one way. But you have to be very specific, and regular, and very attentive to your dreams, so that later on things will verify. All through my life I had dreams of Egypt, some connection with Egypt. When I was a young woman writing for the newspaper in Berlin, for example, I had a dream in which an Egyptian man came to me holding out a tray with a beautiful necklace on it. I admired the necklace and asked him who it was for.

" 'For you,' he said.

" 'Well,' I said, 'That's not possible.'

"Then the Egyptian man said, 'I wonder how many more confirmations you need?'

"So. I wondered about that, too. Where do these ideas come from? The problem was I couldn't discuss these things with anyone. When so many people, women in particular, told me they had been one of the queens of Egypt in a past life, I decided it would be better not to say anything more about my dreams. I didn't want to be lumped in with a group of hysterical women."

Ahead of us lay a vast panorama of coniferous forest broken only by the two-lane highway carrying us westward. Thoughts of past lives and unfinished business filled my mind and I wondered, too, where these ideas come from. Oddly, they did not seem strange to me at all. There was logic and continuity in the idea that we could be born for a purpose that included unfinished tasks from another time, perhaps something that had to be completed before any degree of personal freedom was even possible. Then there was the question of duty and responsibility. How could I know what was mine, and what wasn't? After a long silence, I asked Swami Radha why she had said the North could have something to do with unfinished business.

She thought for a moment before answering.

"Normally it's not logic that would lead me to think of unfinished business. Sometimes it's a feeling or an immediate response that only later is confirmed in some way. We all have something in us that I call the knower—the one that knows, and if you let the knower take over, you might find out what is there. For me it can be quite obvious because I'm not involved in what you're doing. But for you certain things will not be obvious because you've already set your mind on something else.

"I asked you about the challenge, and you didn't have any specific answer to that. In your present life with your background and education and everything else, it doesn't make any sense that you would have a problem getting work, and that you would have to go into the North to make your livelihood. You're not a trapper who can live on game and sell furs or whatever. So there are certain things about the choices you've made that don't make sense. If there is a very strong feeling like the one you just described to me when you went to Donna's house, that can mean there is unfinished business. Have you come back to something that was a dramatic experience? It can be a good dramatic experience; it may even have been wonderful. But it could also have been a negative dramatic experience. Somehow there's still unfinished business.

"You see, there is in some men the adventurer—more in men than in women, although I've seen it in women, too. They seek danger and challenge, the kind of challenges that are extremely difficult if not impossible for others to do, but they do not seek *the* challenge. Now you could be one of those. But why would you do it here? Challenges you can have anywhere. So, basically you've come into the North looking for something. What is it? What is it you're after? Whatever it is, *that* is your true challenge."

We passed a blue road sign announcing a restaurant and gas station ahead. Ah, good, I thought to myself, a chance for a cigarette outside and a few minutes by myself to let some of this sink in.

"You can smoke in the restaurant if you want to," she said, as we turned into the parking lot. "I don't mind. Wolfgang was a smoker and for a few months after I emigrated to Canada, I smoked too. That was a very challenging time in my life.

"But European cigarettes don't have as many chemical additives as the ones made here," she added as I held the door open for her. "Maybe I can find some European cigarettes for you."

～

An hour or so east of Thunder Bay, Swami Radha closed her eyes and dozed off beside me. Outside the temperature was dropping and the sky to the southeast was turning dark. I glanced at my watch. Quarter to five. We had made good time.

What was the unfinished business? The more I thought about it, the more it seemed possible that something beyond my little self had orchestrated the serpentine path leading me back to this place beside her. My thoughts wandered back to 1976 when I first met Donna and Alicia in Thunder Bay. At the time I was getting ready to leave that northern city forever, but forever didn't turn out to be very long. After a few months of living together as a family in Toronto, we decided to move back to the North, this time to her house in Sioux Lookout. We were married in a ceremony that took place just a few feet along the shoreline from where I had first experienced a sense of the mystical power of the land. When I had the experience, the thought that I would be living there a year later never crossed my mind.

Now, driving with Swami Radha across country that had become very important to me, I was starting to put the pieces of my life's journey together and it occurred to me that Swami Radha's Divine Committee idea could be another way of understanding how the power that has created life, what we usually think of as God, is directly involved in the business of looking after its creation. Considering the circumstances that had brought us all together—Donna, Alicia, me, and now Swami Radha—I was starting to think that it is.

Alicia was four and a half years old when I first saw her sitting on her mother's lap in the kitchen of the apartment I rented on the second floor of an old house on Cameron Street in Thunder Bay. Our encounter was brief. It was the first day of my vacation after a long, dark, northern Ontario winter and I was eager to be on the road. My heart was filled with kind feelings towards the mother and daughter who had agreed to sublet my apartment while I was away.

"I'll just take a minute to say goodbye and wish them well," I said to myself as I put my suitcase down by the front door. "Then I shall be on my way."

Unfortunately it wasn't quite that simple. My good intentions were lost on the little girl who burst into tears the moment I entered the kitchen. Her mother hastened to assure me that it had nothing to do with my sudden appearance. Something about not wanting to wear socks, she explained, as I backed out of the room. Perhaps. But the tears made me uncomfortable and I didn't know how to respond. Amidst the wailing, I said my goodbyes, goodlucks, all the bests, hope things get better, maybe new socks—words; and left—down the stairs, running now—free at last. Best to keep moving, I said to myself as I turned the key in the ignition, backed out onto the street, and was gone— down the road, down the road, down the road—until the weight of my indifference caught up to me. Finally I had to pull over to the side of the road, too exhausted to go any further. Cars and huge trucks whooshed by, hurrying to their destinations. As far as I was concerned they could go on without me. Loneliness. Something was calling but I could not hear what it was.

At that time I could not have seen that the steps leading to my marriage and an entirely different focus for my life had already been taken. But Swami Radha's questions spurred me to think about the decisions I'd made and where they had taken me. I wondered, too, at the destiny that had created the circumstances for us to meet. That and the grace that had given us this time together.

It started to rain, just a few drops now but soon it would pick up. Tiny dusty rivulets rolled across the hood of the car and disappeared over the side. The tires felt a little less sure on the slippery road but soon the rain would wash the road clean. If it rained enough everything would come alive with the scent of the forest all around us. Beside me Swami Radha was sleeping.

I love driving in the rain. Six years ago I drove through the night along this same road, coming home from my vacation. It was raining then, too. I'm not sure why it was so important to keep going that night, except that I welcomed the solitude and the darkness and the smell of the rain and I wanted to be in it, not cooped up in some dank, dingy motel room. Now and then, between long silent intervals, road signs would suddenly leap into the headlights from the side of the road, announcing the imminent arrival of the next pulp town along the way. White River, Marathon, Terrace Bay, Red Rock—simple roadside markers defying the anonymity and deadening conformity of towns that are closed to all but the few who are willing to give their lives to the companies that built them. All night long the car radio drifted back and forth across the AM band. Depending on the rise and fall of the landscape, everything from hell-fire and brimstone preachers to howling Chicago blues cried out in the night from the dimly lit center of the dashboard. Across the rolling North Shore highway, none of the sounds stayed with me long enough to become real. Round a bend or descend a long hill and the whole show would drift off into the night.

It was seven in the morning when I turned off the Trans-Canada Highway onto the Arthur Street exit into Thunder Bay. The dawn sky was gray and overcast though there were signs of clearing in the south. I rolled down the window and almost immediately the warm, damp, sulfuric smell of the paper mill out by Neebing filled the car. Donna and Alicia have the only key to my apartment, I thought. If no one's home, I'll have to sit outside and wait. After hurrying so much to get home, this realization made me chuckle and filled me with a feeling of peace.

The woman who greeted me at the door was someone I had never seen before. Her dark eyes flashed with warmth and humor when she saw my surprise.

"You must be David," she said cheerfully. "Donna said you were coming this morning. You don't know me. I'm her friend, Linda. I'm going to help her and Alicia move this morning. Come in. We're just having breakfast."

Alicia was sitting up in bed when I took my bags into the room she and her mom had used while I was away. Her round, bright eyes looked straight at me.

"My leg's asleep," she announced.

"It must need the rest," I replied as I put my bags down.

Deep inside me a warm, relaxed feeling started to dissolve the weariness from the night. A large cardboard box filled to overflowing with brightly colored toys and books sat on the floor in the middle of the room. Tiny blue leotards and a purple T-shirt hung over the edge of the dresser. Underwear and socks were crammed into an open drawer, at least those that had made it to the drawer. I laughed quietly as I bent to pick up a sock. It was good to be home after such a long journey.

After breakfast, I helped load Donna's car while she finished packing inside. When the last box was done, I carried it out to her car. That's when I first noticed the *Jerusalem Bible* on the back seat.

"You...uh...read that stuff?" I asked.

"Yes."

"Um. You like it? Is this a good version?"

"I think so. I've had it for awhile. Linda and I sometimes use it when we pray together."

"Oh. Well, I was just asking. Maybe I could borrow it sometime when you're not using it."

Donna had found an apartment just a few blocks from her job in the radio station where I worked. She's doing pretty well, I thought, as I watched her car disappear around the corner at the bottom of the street. I stood on the sidewalk looking at the old brick houses lining both sides of the street, mostly two-story family dwellings in what had always been a solid, working-class neighborhood. I liked old brick houses and old neighborhoods, although I had never allowed myself to stay very long in any one place. Ever since I had left home when I was eighteen, I had always felt the need to keep moving. I used to say to myself, If I just keep moving I'll be all right, I won't get caught, although I had no idea what it was I thought would catch me. It was an odd kind of restlessness that I had never questioned.

After a few minutes I walked back into the house. Everything was tidy; even the dishes were done. I poured myself a cup of coffee and sat down at the kitchen table. Gradually silence filled the room as the echoes of their voices faded away. I sipped my coffee and looked out the window at the deserted street. A wave of fatigue came over me bringing with it a deep, almost overwhelming sadness. Maybe I need sleep, I thought, and I got up from the table and went down the hall to my room. But I couldn't sleep. I lay on my back staring at the ceiling, but sleep wouldn't come and the sadness remained. Finally I gave up and rolled out of bed. Only then did I notice the small white sock lying next to the wastebasket in the corner of the room.

～

Until our visit with the woman in Thunder Bay who was dying of cancer, I had never seen so clearly how the mind under certain conditions could unconsciously direct the will towards one's own demise. For me, self-will was a powerful manifestation of the instinct for survival. Yet from what I observed in Thunder Bay, the will normally applied to living could indeed be applied to dying.

Colleen was her name. She was a very close friend of Donna's, which is how she had come to meet Swami Radha in the first place. When Donna first heard about Colleen's lymphoma, she invited her to a workshop on spiritual practice given by Swami Radha in Sioux Lookout. The two women had an immediate liking for each other. Swami Radha was very direct with her, perhaps sensing that Colleen didn't have much time. Even so she gave her time to be heard, something Colleen had never had in her marriage. I think Swami Radha admired her spirit, too. It was formidable in the face of tremendous adversity.

Colleen's black hair, which at one time she had worn in long braids like an Ojibway woman, was now patchy and uneven, sacrificed to the chemotherapy that was battling the cancerous cells in her body. But the sparkle in her dark eyes revealed the depth of her happiness at seeing Swami Radha once again. When I saw their warm spontaneity together, it struck me that women could be far more courageous than men in the face of death. Women seem more accepting of death as an integral part of life. I knew from experience that women's compassion could be extremely direct and practical. These thoughts flitted across my mind and quickly disappeared. It was enough to see how the Light in Swami Radha was gathering around Colleen, holding and protecting her, and how quickly she responded to that Light.

Colleen introduced us to her best friend, Betty, who had arranged a morning off from work when she heard that Swami Radha would be visiting. Betty had known her friend since high school but it was only in the last year or so, particularly since the diagnosis of cancer, that she and Colleen had taken their old friendship and forged it into a powerful bond of affection and support. As a single mother of two young children with an alcoholic husband continuing to make emotional demands on her, Colleen needed all the help she could get. Betty provided it. As far as I could tell she was one of the most selfless people I had ever met.

In the end we couldn't stay long. Colleen didn't have a lot of endurance at this stage of her illness, though she kept insisting that she had been doing a lot better since the end of summer. I wasn't an expert at reading the signs but the prospects for Colleen's recovery didn't look promising to me. Swami Radha kept exhorting Colleen to conserve her energy and rest as much as she could.

"You are involved in a battle," she said, "and you must have the energy to fight it."

As I watched their interaction, Colleen gradually began to slow down and pull in, first in her speech, then in her body movements. She had never been one to sit still, always up and looking after others, trying to take care of everybody at once. Yet under Swami Radha's influence she began to calm down and relax. It was like watching a sick child surrender into the care of the mother. But like a child, the moment Colleen started to feel better she would be up looking after us, wanting more than anything to be able to respond to people she cared about in the way that she had all her life. Even Betty, whose job it was to keep her old friend going, had almost to order Colleen to sit down and let her take care of things. I saw the pride dart across Colleen's face as she submitted to her friend's command, and wondered what it was about.

"I have to keep moving," she told Swami Radha, "otherwise my joints begin to tighten up and swell and the pain is terrible. What I'd really like to do is just to be able to walk outside again, even if it is just up and down in front of the house. But I'm afraid of going out if something should happen and I can't get back into my house."

Betty offered a practical solution.

"I can come over from work at lunch hour every day," she said to Colleen. "It's not far and I'd love to be able to see you. We could walk together then."

The sincerity of Betty's offer went right to my heart. Something about the way in which she had made it—straight, open, caring deeply about her friend—left no doubt in my mind that she had meant what she said. Clearly the well-being of her friend took precedence over her own needs. For her it was no sacrifice. What really surprised me was Colleen's response.

"Oh, that would be good," she said, "but you don't have to do that. I can manage okay."

Betty tried again, this time explaining to Colleen that since she liked to use the time to jog anyway she might as well give it a direction, too, and that it was no problem for her at all.

"Well, yes…" said Colleen. "We'll have to see. I'm not sure I'd be up to it."

What's going on? Here this woman was dying and her best friend almost had to plead to be allowed to help. I didn't get it.

"I don't get it," I suddenly burst out. "Don't you want Betty's help? I mean, Colleen, she's offering to help. Not only that, everything Swami Radha has said to you, you've found some way to say no to. Don't you want to get well?"

Swami Radha didn't say anything but she watched Colleen closely. In the silence following my little tirade it dawned on me that there could be another side to sickness, that a sick person could use self-will not to get well if that was the underlying desire. That someone would not want to get well was a new one for me, but then I did not understand much about the mind and how pride and self-will could undermine the desire to live—or if it was even that. Maybe there is such a thing as a life having an allotted time for taking the next step or, as I had recently begun to think, for taking care of unfinished business.

Swami Radha did not get into it. For her the focus was on the Light that was Colleen's only chance. She sat in her chair across from Colleen, filling her with Light, and the whole room, and Betty, and me, until there was almost no resistance left. Then when Colleen was silent at last, Swami Radha went over to Colleen sitting on the couch and sat down beside her. Still without saying a word she took Colleen in her arms and held her while Colleen cried and cried. Although it seemed to go on for a long time, it was really only a few minutes and Colleen was ready for sleep.

"I think this is the first time in weeks that I feel I can rest without having to take a sleeping pill," she told Swami Radha. "I feel so relaxed now."

Colleen lay down on the couch and Betty carefully spread a soft woolen blanket over her friend. The atmosphere in the house was so peaceful now, so unlike what it had been when we came in. We left Colleen sleeping on the couch and went out into the front hall. At the door, Swami Radha took Betty's hand and told her that she was very good for her friend and that she must make sure Colleen did everything possible to conserve her energy. The two women hugged briefly and then we left. It was only about 12:30 in the afternoon. As we walked to the car I told Swami Radha that I thought we could easily be in Sioux Lookout by suppertime, particularly since we would pass through a time zone and gain an hour along the way.

CHAPTER SIX

Maze

Until the Music and Consciousness workshop with Swami Radha
that weekend in Sioux Lookout, I had not given any serious
thought to the possibility that my life might be part of a larger
divine plan, that it could have a purpose larger than personal gratification and success. It was not only a question of knowing how to see the
larger view, but also whether or not I was willing to stop long enough
to look once I knew how. That part I wasn't so sure of. On the opening
night of the workshop, Swami Radha asked us to reflect on the number
of times divine intervention—Divine Mother—had either protected us
from our own ignorance or opened the way for taking the next step,
and if we were willing to see ourselves at the gut level in order to find
out what that step might be. The question demanded serious reflection. I had been thinking a lot about my relationship to the Divine
since our trip together. In fact the whole spiritual dimension of my life
was under scrutiny. By the time our group gathered together Friday
night to do the exercise for the workshop, I was keyed up with
anticipation.

The Music and Consciousness workshop came at a point in our
marriage when Donna and I were struggling to rise above the stubbornness and self-will that was slowly cementing our differences into a
wall of anger and resistance—she to me, I to her. Resistance (read pride)
was tearing us apart. Finally we arrived at a critical juncture.

Donna said, "Either you do something about your emotions, or this
marriage ends."

I remember standing in the kitchen of our house staring at her in amazement. How could she say such a thing, she who had relied almost exclusively on her emotions over reason in every confrontation between us? I was speechless.

I remained speechless for the rest of the day and through the night until early the next morning when Alicia, playing by herself before breakfast, happened to fly a favorite model airplane of mine into the living room wall. Upon impact the plane disintegrated into a hundred pieces. As I surveyed the wreckage scattered across the floor, I recalled the many hours that had gone into the construction of this beautifully painted, meticulously detailed World War Two fighter plane. Now, having encountered unyielding resistance, my painstaking efforts lay in ruin before my eyes. I reached down to pick up a piece of broken plastic and caught a faint glimmer of the absurd through a crack in the wall of my pride.

"Am I willing to pay the price of this marriage and family in order to preserve my pride?" I wondered.

In that moment I made a pact with myself to do whatever was necessary to save our marriage. The Music and Consciousness workshop was among the early steps.

Through intensive mantra practice, Swami Radha had learned that thoughts and images (along with their emotional colorings) are called forth from the unconscious part of mind through the power of sound and vibration. Memories, old desires, aversions, unfinished business, attachments, childhood experiences, singular events, sometimes strange unfamiliar shapes and forms perhaps originating far back in time—all reside in the unconscious mind like the contents of a cosmic storage bin. Introduce a precise rate of vibration—a tone of voice, your name, the name of a close friend, an old song, a single note—and they come to life. Like dreams they are often perplexing, even mystifying, in the absence of logic and reason.

The exercise preceding the workshop involves listening to seven pieces of music and drawing the images that arise in the mind after each piece on a large sheet of blank newsprint using simple wax crayons. When the drawings are done you lay them out on the floor in a row in the order in which you drew them. What you're looking at is a symbolic representation of your path through life—as it has been, as it is now, and even how it might be in the future. To understand this, the pictures as symbols need to be translated into the language of the intellect using logic and reason together with an intuitive questioning process.

What amazes me today is the connection between those drawings made almost twenty years ago and what has transpired since. At the time of the workshop, Swami Radha advised me to keep a record, a spiritual diary. Today, seeing the creative power of mind at work through the accumulated record of my diaries, I am very grateful to her for making that suggestion. Without the record, I would never have believed how selective and malleable memory can be when it comes to sustaining a preferred image of myself. The ego uses everything, including memory, to present itself in a favorable light.

On the first night of the workshop, we listened to selections from a broad range of music, starting with Vivaldi's "Four Seasons," then moving to the sound of Chinese bells or what could have been a glockenspiel, and on through the other pieces until the haunting resonance of the Hari Om mantra concluded the exercise. One by one I made my drawings and in the process found myself going deeper and deeper as if a sleeping part of my mind was gradually awakening to the vibrations calling me inward. That I was taking the first step towards a new life, away from the bush and the land I had become so attached to, never occurred to me.

Two of my drawings, particularly, span the years with their prophetic power. The first, drawn to the sound of the Chinese bells, was the image of a child's maze similar to the ones I'd seen on the back pages of comic books when I was a kid. To solve the problem of how to draw a maze that actually worked, I drew the path first, then put the maze around it afterwards. It was the only way I could think of to convey the image I had seen in my mind while listening to the sound, but the next day in the workshop when I explained the process to Swami Radha, she looked at me acutely; then turned to the others in the room.

"Well, who can hear the message he has just given to himself? Who can hear it?" she asked.

Someone said, "He knows the path."

"Right. He drew the path before drawing the maze over it. What does that say? That the soul came into this life with a very determined idea, and that life put the maze on afterwards. That's what it is."

Her eyes shone with great kindness, but the tone of her voice left no doubt of the seriousness of what she was saying.

"Now, whether your stubborn little mind can accept this," she said, "is a different matter. If you do, you could have very smooth sailing in this life. The path is clear; you've marked it in red which shows clearly where it is. The green color around it is life itself, like the prana, your own life force.

"Tara and the Buddha are often shown with a red halo which is different from the white halos of Christianity. Halos represent Higher Consciousness, and in order to achieve that Higher Consciousness you have to direct all of your passion into the search for it. The path of Awareness has to be pursued with the same passion that you would bring to the pursuit of anything else you wanted badly enough. Passion should not be suppressed or meddled with. It should just be given the right direction, just as you've done with your map here. The mind, the intellect, constructs whatever it can to make you appear better or different or whatever. The unconscious, on the other hand, usually speaks the truth and it is your unconscious, David, that has presented you with this map. The question is: Can you accept it?"

Could I accept anything from a woman was the underlying challenge posed by her question. As a man I had never been taught to think beyond what was intellectually acceptable according to my powers of reasoning. What wasn't rational—emotions, feelings, thoughts that

defied reason—my intellect easily dismissed with the surety of arrogance. Now, through the language of the pictures, I was trying to enter
in and listen, and it wasn't easy. Swami Radha must have sensed this
because that's what she spoke to next.

"I'm sure, David, in your conscious mind you have occasionally
played around with certain ideas. But men's logic and reason do not
permit those ideas to emerge. In our country men don't do workshops
like this. They think it's fine for women and that's why you find more
women in workshops and churches. However, in the East it's the other
way around. Among the hundreds of men that my guru initiated, there
were only five women initiated into mantra, and only two into sanyas.
Here in the West, the man hides his intuitive feelings, his ability for
intuitive thinking and listening. In the East, the intuitive is much more
an active part of people's lives; at least, that is how it has been in the
past. Of course, now the East is losing this, too.

"Think about it, David. This may be the answer to many of the
contradictions you find inside yourself when you are in the abyss of
depression. The depression comes about because you don't really understand yourself. But here is your map. It came directly from your
own mind. I didn't say, 'David, here's your plan. I've mapped it all out
for you, and all you have to do is accept it.' No. It came from you, from
yourself. And when it comes from the unconscious, it is the safest way
for you to get the message."

All that came from one drawing, made from the simple tinkling
sound of Chinese bells.

The other drawing that seemed most significant to me was of a
large black boulder sitting in the middle of a dirt road. The boulder
occupied most of the road making it impossible to pass. Swami Radha
sat forward in her chair looking thoughtfully at the drawing on the
floor. Then she straightened up and looked at me with a big smile.

"Ah," she said. "Do you remember on our trip when you described
the little black bear on the road? And you stopped?"

I did remember. It happened one day during the summer when I was coming out of the bush with a full load of pulpwood. I was just coming over the crest of a long hill when a little bear cub ran out of the bush onto the road at the bottom of the hill, sat down in the middle of the road, and started to scratch himself furiously. Normally that would not have presented a problem. But I had more than twenty cords of wood on the trailer and I knew with that much weight coming down the hill behind me it would be impossible to stop in time. I tried, though. With the horn blaring and the air brakes locked on, I was down to less than thirty feet from the little bear when he suddenly stopped scratching, looked up, and at the very last second bounded off the road and up the bank on the other side. When I finally got the truck stopped, well past where he had been sitting, I jumped down and ran back up the road to see if I could spot him. He hadn't gone far. I looked up the bank and into the eyes of the little black cub staring down at me from his elevated perch, waiting to see what would happen next. It crossed my mind that perhaps he did this every day just to scare the hell out of logging truck drivers and I started to laugh. It was a beautiful sunny day. No one else was around—just me and the little bear, and the bush surrounding us, absolutely still under the hot noonday sun.

That's the story Swami Radha was referring to. Because the whole episode had drawn me into the natural world in such an intimate and affectionate way, I had told her about it when she had asked me on our trip why anyone would want to live in the northern bush. My drawing of the black boulder in the road had reminded her of the story, only now she was able to take its meaning to the next stage.

"You had to stop your truck," she said, "which is the mind. Here you have to stop the mind, and climb over in good faith, and you cannot take the mind with you to the other side."

Again she turned to the rest of the people in the room.

"Isn't it amazing? If you allow yourself to really think about it, you'll see that his unconscious is making a tremendous effort to give him the message so that he can pursue it. I think it's incredible. If you can just see it, you're getting a message here, David, from Divine Law. Only if you ignore it or let it go will you encounter trouble. It's not falling into occasional temptation that makes one a sinner. Even if a person has a fling, that is nature and God knows that, too. No. Simply denying that you ever got the message makes you the sinner. That is what Jesus meant in the New Testament when he said, 'All sins are forgiven except the sin against the Holy Spirit.' That is the message of the Holy Spirit. Once that message comes from your own inner being you cannot deny it, and it will confirm itself over and over. Most people get that message only once on a single sheet of paper and it can sometimes be very faint. But you have it here, on one sheet after the other: bang, bang, bang! So, what is the obstacle?"

I knew it had something to do with my willingness to go ahead on the spiritual path but I couldn't express that clearly in the moment. Instead, I described the difficulty I'd had with chanting the Hari Om mantra I had learned in the course at her ashram, and the constriction as my throat inevitably tightened around the high C. What made the problem more than just a matter of voice training was the fact that every time I sang the mantra, I would become almost overwhelmed with anxiety and tension within a few minutes of starting. Then my throat would constrict, my breathing would grow shallow and I'd have to stop. That was how I explained the obstacle in the road.

Swami Radha referred to Saint Paul in the New Testament.

"Daily I die," she said. "What do you think Saint Paul meant by those words? Self-will. The monkey mind says, 'No, we're not going to sing Hari Om. No. I want to have the crown on *my* head. *I* want to be worshipped. *I* want to be recognized.' It's the monkey mind that Saint Paul was referring to. Daily I die. Daily he had to slay self-will. And he also said, 'I have my life only in Christ.' By that he meant, only in Higher Consciousness. Everything else is an illusion.

"The boulder in your road is an obstacle, perhaps unfinished business. You have to remove that obstacle so that other people can walk smoothly over the same road that you are walking. It is very hard to accept these things but the responsibility is yours. Somebody has to fill in the holes and remove the boulders. Just allow yourself to be a divine instrument, and do not care what anyone says in their judgment of you. The time will come when you can say, 'I know God is up here,' " —she pointed to her head—"and later you will know that God is here"—she pointed to her heart—"and you won't care what anybody says.

"What is important? That I have God's love. That is what is important. Your love for me, the love of all of you put together, is very small and it will fizzle out the moment I don't do your bidding. But Divine Love will never leave me. My life may sometimes be like a dark cloud hiding that love and I may not see it. But there is a knowing in the heart that love is there, and as with any weather, you wait for the currents to recede. The sun appears, the Light is here again. It's the same thing with Divine Love. At the time of death all your achievements, all your successes, mean nothing. Consciousness? Yes, that you can take with you. Consciousness is what survives. If I look at this drawing as your physical self and your Divine Self, I can see sparks going between them, and that's good! You can turn any negative into the positive, David. The boulder is simply blocking your unfulfilled potential."

We took a break at that point and I went outside for a walk. My emotions were stirred up and I had a lot to think about. Swami Radha had challenged me, or more precisely, my unconscious mind had challenged me, and she had been the vehicle for delivering the message. I couldn't figure out quite what was happening except that I was feeling highly charged, excited—happy, I suppose, though the word seemed barely adequate to describe the depth of feeling coursing through me and around me. There was no doubt in my mind that something important had been awakened from the workshop, from our trip together, or maybe it was the influence of the Light she kept referring to. She had mentioned unfinished business again, but at least now I had an image to go with the metaphor of my life as a journey with a profound purpose. What am I supposed to do now? I wondered as I walked back towards the house. Whatever it is, why am I drawn to it now when I have so much? As profound as my experience had been with Swami Radha in the workshop, I now felt the resistance in me beginning to take hold. I was anxious and worried about what would happen next, though I had no conscious idea of what that was going to be.

"Everything has speeded up," I said to Donna as I sat down in the chair beside her.

Across from us, just as Swami Radha was getting ready to start again, a ray of afternoon sun came through the window and turned her silver-white hair into amber-gold. In that moment I was almost overwhelmed with feelings of gratitude for her. I knew in that moment beyond any doubt that she was the most compassionate and intelligent person I had ever met.

Swami Radha began by asking Donna to put her drawings on the floor beside mine. Then she asked us both to look at the drawings side by side. Almost at once the two paths symbolized by the drawings began to merge and I was amazed to see how similar they were. For one piece of music, the sound of a single drumbeat, we had both drawn the same symbol—the continent of Africa with a large orange disk at its center—though neither of us had seen what the other was drawing. I was struck by other similarities, as well, and I began to consider again the person I had married. Did I really know her? Did I even know myself? Apparently not as well as I had supposed.

As we continued to look over our drawings it soon became evident to both of us that we were far more than our personality aspects, especially those stubborn unyielding ones that were turning a happy marriage into a dark cell of conflict and doubt. I reasoned that if our paths were as similar as they appeared to be, then our marriage had a very different purpose than either of us had supposed.

Swami Radha pointed out that our marriage could be the means through which our individual consciousnesses would evolve, if we were willing to cooperate with the forces of evolution that had brought us together, and if we were willing to help each other move towards the goal of Higher Consciousness that our drawings had clearly shown to be identical. Her "mountain analogy," as I called it, lifted our marriage out of its familiar emotional context to a larger, more realistic and much more hopeful perspective. She explained it to us by folding a handkerchief into the shape of a triangle. Then placing it on her knee, she pointed to the base of the triangle.

"You, David, are here," she said, indicating one end of the base, "and, Donna, you are here," indicating the other end. "Now you meet and go towards each other and eventually decide you want to get married. After you marry you keep traveling towards each other along this same line, continuing to put your focus and your expectations onto each other. But you see, this won't work. The male and the female are opposites. What is needed is a goal, a focus outside of this two-way, back-and-forth movement that is not going anywhere. If you put your focus here," she said, indicating the third point at the top of the triangle, "that can be your goal, the top of the mountain. Your work together, then, is to help each other get to the top. Now if that mountain is Higher Consciousness you can see how much that would affect your expectations of each other, and perhaps you can begin to see that your marriage may have come about for a purpose very different from what you thought at the beginning.

"And remember," she concluded, "no two individual people climb the same mountain in precisely the same way, nor do they ascend at the same pace. At one time he may be slightly ahead, at another time she will be, but the one is always aware of the other and ready to help when the need arises. There are steep, hard places going almost straight up, but there are also gently rolling pathways where you can stop and rest and take in the magnificent view. You both are on the same mountain but you each will have your own way of getting to the top. Your job in this lifetime is to help each other get there. Om Om."

Here Swami Radha brought her palms together at her heart, her pranam to both of us. The gesture is more familiar in the East but it means "The Divine in me salutes the Divine in you." For the first time in years I felt full and my mind was quiet. The door had opened to new possibilities for both of us and the time for crossing the threshold was fast approaching.

~

Monday morning after the workshop I left the house around 4:30 and headed north out of Sioux Lookout, back to the bush where I had a log hauling contract to fulfill. In the faint morning light the gray sky appeared overcast but the temperature was warmer than it had been for the past few days. I was barely through town before the first raindrops splattered across the truck's windshield. I didn't mind. The air was sweet and I was feeling happy and full as I crossed the bridge over Sturgeon River and turned up the hill on the other side of the railway tracks running along the bank of the river. If you happened to be coming down that same hill and knew where to look, you'd see a small wooden cross in the tall grass off to your right between the road and the tracks. Local people said the cross marked the spot where a Chinese railway worker was buried after he dropped dead while working on the construction of the railroad at the turn of the century. They told me that by the time the railway was completed you could find crosses like this one along the whole length of track from one end of the country to the other. Whether it was true about the Chinese man or the crosses I couldn't say. It was just one of those incontestable "facts" locals everywhere swear to as if they'd been there and seen the whole thing themselves right down to the actual burying. But the truth of the story didn't matter so much. After I heard it I could never again cross those tracks without shivering slightly at the thought of those bones right there in the ground beside me as I rolled past.

At the top of the hill I shifted from mid to high range and accelerated along the uneven stretch of blacktop ahead. The rain was really coming down now and I wondered about Swami Radha's flight to Winnipeg. There was no way it would get off the ground if the rain didn't let up soon. I looked at my watch. 5:15. Still lots of time for the weather to clear before she was supposed to leave. I thought about our trip together across the North Shore. It was only three weeks ago that we had left Toronto but it seemed almost like another lifetime. She had been great fun to travel with, that was true, but far more than fun had come from our time together. Now it was over. In just a few hours she would be on her way home to the ashram in British Columbia, and I would be coming out of the bush on my way to the mill in Thunder Bay. Still, something in me had changed. I could feel it though I didn't have the language to explain it. A lot had been stirred up for me in the last few weeks and I needed this time to think about my life and to try to make sense of the maze it had been until now.

Swami Radha's question about Divine Mother's protection kept coming back to me—that and the maze drawing on my Music and Consciousness. Yes, She had been there all along protecting me from my own ignorance, protecting me from dangers real and imagined, and ironically, even going so far as to disguise Herself as an illusion—the maze of life itself—to shield me from the glare of Her awesome creative power. I had never thought about this protective power of God as being feminine, particularly in the form of the mother. The image of mother, though ambiguous for me, was nevertheless a starting place for forming a different kind of relationship with the Divine.

So how had She worked in my life?

The first thought that came to me was of a dream I had thirty years ago, the morning after my parents were killed in a car accident. I was twenty-two at the time. In the dream they appeared before me, all bruised and cut up and bloody, and they were saying over and over to me, "We are all right. You will be all right, too. Don't worry."

The dream was so real I jolted awake and cried out, "Oh! It's just a dream. They're alive. I've been dreaming the whole thing."

But even as my words tumbled into the darkness I felt the pain returning, bringing with it the sadness that sleep had temporarily held at bay. For years after whenever I recalled that dream I would get angry because to me it had been such a cruel deception. Now I think about it again, and I begin to see that the dream had all the grace of Her protection.

My parents had already been dead for twelve hours when the fellows I shared a house with at university came to the hotel where I worked part-time to tell me about the accident. I remember us standing in the parking lot outside the hotel bar as if it was yesterday, and one of my friends saying, "…killed in a car accident." His words hit me on the side of the head like a heavy club.

I fell back onto the hood of a car, crying out, "No! That's wrong! You're trying to make a joke…it's not funny. What're you trying to do?" and then the shock ripped through me like a bolt of lightning in the night.

Tears and anger seemed to flow together after that. I remember running back into the hotel, through the Saturday night crowd and up to the cash register at the end of the bar where I tried to cash in my waiter's float—twenty dollars in change and small bills. My hands shook and I couldn't see through the tears to count the money. I kept having to start over again until finally, in exasperation, I threw all the loose change I had onto the counter and turned to leave. Out of the corner of my eye, I saw the bartender nod as he watched the coins skid across the glistening wooden surface and into the stainless steel sink below.

"Keep moving. Just keep moving," I said to myself. "I'll be all right. Just don't stop."

This is what I said to get through that night. I sat slumped in the passenger seat of my own car as we turned onto the highway and headed east, back to where it had all started for me, back to where I used to live, to where my parents used to live. Someone else was driving my car. Why would anyone think I couldn't drive my own car? This is ridiculous. No one knows this car as well as I do. No one!

"Runs good at night," I blurted into the darkness. "It's the carburetor," I added, as my brain finally latched onto something real. "Four-barrel. Likes the moisture in the air."

I stared at the road ahead, watching the lights of other cars approaching while I breathed in the warm smell of engine oil and listened to the reassuring sound of valves and pistons moving together.

"Reliable," I said to myself. "Steady and reliable."

Gradually the numbing aftermath of shock closed in. My eyes grew heavy and sleep arrived to shut down the pain.

Later that night after my friends had left, I sat alone in my parents' house and tried to think things through. I was frightened by what had happened, at how fast death can change everything. In a split second the two people I had known all my life and the structure I called family ceased to exist. Surrender seemed to be the only reasonable response, accepting what had happened, letting go, allowing others to take care of details I couldn't even think about. I was not used to letting anybody take care of things that I felt were my responsibility, but death had never before come this close and I didn't know what else to do. That night I had the dream about my parents.

During our trip, Swami Radha had alluded several times to the protection of Divine Mother in her own life—from the family cook who looked after her when she was a child to the protection that came to her over and over during the war. She even referred to her own guru, Swami Sivananda, as her spiritual mother and told me that she had experienced his protection many times. So the dream for me was an example of a protection that I could trust. I knew that now. But there were other things, too—Mrs. Robinson, for example. She and her son, Harry.

I met Harry Robinson a few months after my parents died when I went to his church in downtown Toronto, just a block from the city's warehouse district. It was late autumn. Already the trees were bare and the cold wind blowing off Lake Ontario seemed impatient for winter.

A friend had said to me, "Why don't you come to my church? I think you would really like the minister."

I doubted that and said so, but in the end I went because loneliness and sadness were starting to consume me and something needed to change.

Reverend Robinson was a big man, shaggy and slightly disheveled-looking with his bushy eyebrows and thick black hair. His soft, dark brown eyes looked straight into mine when we were introduced and I quickly glanced away, not wanting him to see how vulnerable I had become. But then later, during his sermon, I was drawn to a quality in his speech that seemed to stir an almost forgotten resonance within me. So respectful was he of the power of speech that he would often pause for what seemed an inordinate length of time to find the words that would most accurately and clearly express his deepest thoughts. To me he seemed more concerned about the truth of what he was saying than what its effect might be on his listeners. When I realized that his speech was reflecting his own experience, I finally knew what truth sounds like. It was a startling discovery.

I was still wondering about Harry Robinson when I said goodbye to him at the church door after the service. He smiled at me.

"Are you coming to the farm next weekend for the retreat?" he asked.

I thanked him, declining politely as I turned away from his warmth and openness. Sometime during the week, though, I changed my mind and called the church office.

"Yes. Please sign me up for the weekend," I said to the church secretary.

When a couple of friends of mine heard about it they said I wasn't myself. They were right.

It rained heavily during the trip down to Prince Edward County, and it was still raining hard late that night when we turned off a secondary road onto the gravel lane leading up to the old farmhouse. The "farm" turned out to be the original Robinson family farm in the southern part of the county, close to Lake Ontario. Harry's mother still lived in the house where she'd raised her eight children. Three of the boys including Harry were clerics in the Anglican church. As we drove up the lane towards the house, the trees along both sides of the lane bent to greet us in the driving wind.

Having raised eight children, Mrs. Robinson was clearly experienced at making large groups of people feel right at home. She took charge immediately.

"Coats here, boots over there. Come in, come in, you'll find tea and biscuits on the tray by the fire. Quite a storm, isn't it? We often get them here this time of year. Off the lake, you know."

I entered her warm, active nest and was drawn to the nurturance she had prepared for us. I remember thinking, I will just relax and go with whatever is happening. I will follow and see where this is taking me. I have not been in a warm house for such a long, long time and I do not want ever to go into the cold, black night again.

Mrs. Robinson stood in the center of her living room and welcomed everyone, her voice clear and confident—straight like her son's.

"I am glad you are all safely here after your long journey," she said. "You'll be staying with families from our parish who have offered to billet you for the weekend. Mary, you'll be with the McKuens. John, you're to go with the Browns. Sheila, you're doubling up with Sarah...." I watched the named ones, shy at first, then smiling, eager to overcome the habitual reserve that is common between strangers meeting for the first time. I waited for my name to be called. Mrs. Robinson finished her list and looked around the room until her eyes met mine.

"You, David, will be staying here," she said.

And that was it. Around me people got up to leave, quieter now, settling into themselves, knowing that their accommodation was secure.

I sat watching all this, saying nothing, wondering who this extraordinary woman could be and how it came to pass that I should be the one who got to stay at her house. Beside me the fire burned low in the grate, the room grew quiet, and then seemed to wrap around me like a soft woolen blanket. Mrs. Robinson, frugal and practical by nature, put out all the lights in the room but one, and brought the tray of tea and biscuits to where I was sitting near the fire. She settled herself into the large easy chair across from me and began to pour the tea.

"I danced with your father at my graduation," she said, putting her cup down on the table beside her. "I was eighteen then. Your father was a very good dancer. We grew up together, you know. Do you like cream and sugar in your tea? Are you doing all right, David? I was so sorry to hear about your parents. I never knew your mother but I am certain she must have been a very fine person. Did you know that your grandmother—that would be your father's mother—was married in Harry's church?"

I don't remember our conversation after that. I just remember feeling immense relief. Here was a close witness to my father's life before I knew him, who possibly knew more about him than I ever did. I didn't ask for more; I just wanted this moment between us to go on and on, until my father's life had come full circle. Otherwise, death made no sense at all. Time and memory filled the room and the tension I'd carried since my parents' death began to loosen and drift away. That night I went to sleep in an old feather bed—down, down, into the arms of the Mother who had looked after me all my life. Through my window I could see broken clouds drifting across the face of the moon. The wind softened to a whisper. I slept.

CHAPTER SEVEN

Road to the Light

In the months following my parents' death, perhaps out of a need to protect myself against further shock, I closed down more and more and grew increasingly reluctant to reveal much about myself to anyone. The church retreat weekend at the Robinson family farm, one of the few exceptions to this pattern, had been a profoundly healing experience. One other exception was my brief foray into choral singing, an experience that under normal circumstances would never have happened.

Inspired by an ad in the *Globe and Mail*, the same friend who had taken me to Harry Robinson's church submitted my name for an audition with the Toronto Mendelssohn Choir, then promptly forgot about it. A week later when I received a card in the mail informing me of the time and place for my audition, she was as much taken by surprise as I was. However, my response was considerably less enthusiastic. The audition was a week away and I had never been able to read more than two or three consecutive notes of music in my life.

"Never mind," she said, overriding my concerns. "I know a song from beginning to end and I'll teach it to you. You just go to the audition and sing the song and they'll love it."

For her this was clearly an inspired solution to the problem and to show me how simple it was going to be, she sang the first line of the song.

"Down yonder green valley where streamlets meander...."

That's all I remember. The rest, thankfully, I have forgotten. Yet what emerged from such unlikely beginnings will remain with me for the rest of my life.

I arrived at Grace Church on the Hill, where the auditions were to be held, at the appointed time along with eighty other aspiring choristers most of whom, I soon found out, knew how to read music. Not only that but they had come prepared to sing it. Everyone but I entered the church hall that night with music sheets clutched tightly in hand from a score that was obviously part of the choir's spring repertoire. These people, being old hands in the choir, would have known that and had probably been practicing diligently for weeks. I decided that the best thing for me to do when it came time for my audition would be to introduce myself politely, explain that there had been an unfortunate mistake, apologize profusely for wasting everybody's time by even showing up, and then leave as fast as I could. At quarter past seven my name was called.

"Well, not so fast," the choir director said when I turned to leave. "Have a look at this and see what you think," and he handed me a music sheet that was so dense with black notes I was speechless.

According to the title at the top of the sheet it was the "Lachrymosa" of the Berlioz *Requiem* but apart from that I had no idea what I was looking at. The director looked at me closely then turned to his accompanist seated at the piano and asked her to play the first eight bars.

"Let him hear it," he said. "He'll pick it up then and we'll have some idea of what we have here."

And that's how I ended up singing the first eight bars of the "Lachrymosa" from the Berlioz *Requiem* for my audition. When it was over I thanked the director, apologized again, and departed quickly. Outside, I started to breathe again as the cool night air dried the sweat on my forehead. The thought that maybe I should start looking for a new friend crossed my mind.

But I was missing the point. It was all part of the divine play that was restoring my world by revealing a larger dimension of death. A week after my so-called audition, a card came in the mail informing me that I had been accepted into the choir and that practice would begin within the week. A Bloor Street address and the practice time were noted at the bottom of the card. For the next six months, Monday nights from seven to nine became the most important time of the week for me, the time when I had to force myself out of the sadness and confusion long enough to be a part of the living again. Not only that, but to join with others in singing a requiem mass, a glorious celebration of the crucifixion and ascension of Christ. I learned my part by following the music sheets while listening to a recording of the *Requiem* which I played over and over again. Finally I could recognize the different choral parts that we were working to bring together harmoniously every Monday night. The best part of this method was being able to listen to the "Sanctus" over and over. Every time the tenor voice soared to the climax of the "Terre na," Christ's departure from earth, my spirits would rise in happiness at being in the midst of a group of people working to create something so beautiful and moving for others.

All through that winter and into spring, the choir with just over a hundred members would gather every Monday night to practice the Berlioz *Requiem*. With the approach of Easter we started practicing two nights a week, then three nights, until Good Friday—the night we presented the *Requiem* to a sold-out audience at Varsity Arena. At our last practice before the concert the director, in front of the whole choir, presented me with a bottle of scotch for selling more tickets than anyone else in the room. Everyone applauded enthusiastically but, as I said to them that night, I would have bought the tickets myself just for the privilege of being part of such a moving experience.

Similar to my experience with Mrs. Robinson, all this came about through a power that was not of my own will or choosing. From my perspective, the form these ultimately healing experiences took appeared more circumstantial than intentional. On my own I would not have turned to the church or to any Christian ideology in whatever form it appeared. Yet it kept happening and always I was taken by surprise at the power of the resulting experiences. From my early adolescence as an altar boy in the local Anglican church to the year following my parents' death when I was twenty-two, it had been through the Christian forms that I was drawn more and more towards the Light, though I would not have known to call it that at the time. Yet how else could I describe the messages that were being given to me over and over from as long ago as I could remember.

~

On a cold, rainy Sunday afternoon in London, a week or so after Christmas, 1963, I walked the streets of this ancient, dignified city trying to get rid of a terrible loneliness that had crept into my bones in the last few weeks. It was just over a year since I had left home in Canada, right after my eighteenth birthday, and taken the CN rail east to Sydney, Cape Breton, looking to find a boat that I could work across the Atlantic to Europe. A shipping agent in Sydney worked it out with the captain of a Norwegian pulp freighter bound for Italy.

"You can work as a regular deck hand in exchange for passage," he said to me in his office as he fidgeted through the pile of schedules littering his desk.

"Just make sure you stay out of trouble," he added, looking up just long enough to convey a bit of fatherly concern.

His concern was understandable. I had left home with no thought of going back until I had some idea of what I was going to do with the rest of my life. School was done for me, that was not an option—or so I thought then—and I planned to be gone for two years, maybe longer, depending on how things were working out. With a hundred and ninety-six dollars of summer earnings in my pocket, I assured the agent of my willingness to stay out of trouble.

"Grab your stuff then," he said, "and I'll give ya a ride down to Eskasoni where they're loading out of the bay there. You should be away by tomorrow afternoon if the weather don't change for the worse."

Some of the boldness I had needed to put my own plan into action started to fade as I stood on the ship's deck a few hours later and watched a loading crane yank a bundle of pulp logs out of the floating boom and swing them over the deck and into a hold. Someone had told me that it was not unusual for a ship to lose up to twenty percent of its deck cargo in the fierce storms that sweep across the North Atlantic in winter. I felt my hands tighten on the rail as I visualized an endless string of logs floating aimlessly around the ocean. Across the bay the dense forest crowded the Cape Breton shoreline and again I felt the cold fear that had been with me almost continuously since leaving home. It must have been the fear that prompted me to turn to the wiry Norwegian standing beside me and ask him the one question no one in his right mind would ever ask a sailor.

"Do you have church service on Sundays when you're on the ocean?" I asked, smiling pleasantly.

He turned and looked at me rather strangely, his cold, slightly rheumy blue eyes absolutely expressionless.

"No," he said, and walked away leaving me standing at the railing feeling like an idiot.

For the life of me I could not figure out where the question had come from.

For three days after that none of the crew spoke to me no matter how friendly I tried to be. We weighed anchor and sailed on schedule, which meant that I had work to do, and I figured that once they could see that I was willing and capable, they'd thaw a bit. But it didn't happen. Somehow in a contained vessel at sea with only each other to look at, I had achieved almost total invisibility.

On the third night, well past the Grand Banks of Newfoundland, I was lying on my bunk reading when I heard loud laughter coming from the recreation room off the end of the galley. I got up to see what was happening and found half a dozen sailors playing what looked to me like three-card-draw stud poker. They were all talking Norwegian with an occasional English word, but I was pretty sure I'd recognize the game in any language.

"Can you deal me in?" I asked, big smile on my face.

Stunned silence. The men looked at each other without a word. Finally the second officer spoke up.

"But you're a priest," he said. "You wouldn't want to be playing cards with us."

"A priest?" I said, barely able to believe what I'd heard. "Where did you get that idea? What makes you think I'm a priest?"

The second officer got a bit flustered.

"Well, the first mate told us. He said you were a priest and that you wanted to hold church services on board."

Ah, so that's what had happened at the railing that day. I burst into laughter.

"I'm about as far from the priesthood as you can get," I said with great relief as I sat down to wait for the cards to come around.

And that was my initiation into the world of men. Three weeks later in the northern Italian port of Spezia, I bid a fond, sodden farewell to the men who had belatedly but willingly accepted me into their company.

I boarded the train for England and a week later found a job in London. There I stayed for the next two and a half years.

It sounds exciting and adventurous, and there were times when it was. But mostly I was broke and anxious. A lot of time and effort went into just taking care of basic needs—eating, getting to and from work, trying to set aside enough each week to cover the rent—mundane concerns that didn't leave much room for discovering my life's true vocation.

The loneliness and confusion of that time reached its melancholy peak on that cold, rainy Sunday afternoon in January. I remember staring out the window of my rented room off Bayswater Road at the glistening black asphalt on the deserted street below and saying to myself, "I've got to do something, anything, to break the spell of this depressing state of mind."

I did the only thing I could think of—I walked.

It was late in the afternoon and the streets were deserted. Even the ubiquitous London cabs had disappeared. As I walked along Oxford Street, it suddenly hit me that on this particularly cold, wet Sunday afternoon I happen to have one of the world's most cosmopolitan cities almost entirely at my disposal. The thought was momentarily uplifting, until I counted the loose change in my pocket and remembered that it was all I had to get me through the next day. Two shillings. . . four. . . sixpence. . . that's it. I slid the coins through my fingers once again to make sure. Better keep going, I said to myself as I passed by St. Paul's cathedral and turned south along Fleet Street towards the Embankment. On either side of me long, dark shadows moved in and out of the closed shops and offices lining the empty street.

Halfway down Fleet Street I started to get a feeling that I should turn around and look back. I didn't know where the feeling was coming from but as I turned, a blazing golden-orange light suddenly broke through the heavy winter sky and showered the dome of St. Paul's in a beautiful, soft, golden sheen. The street below the great cathedral lay in darkness. A moment or two later the black clouds of winter closed in again but the image was burned indelibly into my mind. As I started to walk back up the street out of the darkness towards the cathedral, tears warmed the icy rain on my cheeks, washing away the loneliness that had taken up too much space in my heart.

~

In the period after the Music and Consciousness workshop, I continued to think a lot about the play of the Light and Divine Mother's protection in my life. I wondered what my next step with Swami Radha's teachings would be. In the weeks preceding the workshop, Donna had said a number of times that she wanted to take the three-month Yoga Development Course at the ashram in January. After the workshop she mentioned it again and wondered if I would be interested in doing it too.

"I can't," I said. "It's not possible in the winter when the log haul is at its peak. That's when I can make the money that will carry us through the rest of the year. You know that."

I said this thinking it made sense but at the same time there was no mistaking the defensive tone in my voice. The thing was I didn't want to be pressured into taking a step I was not ready to take. That was the truth of it and the rationalization made me feel better even though I knew it was only partly true. But I also knew that if I was willing to listen to the part of my mind that had responded to the Light that summer I met Swami Radha, I would know what was really true and what I ought to do. It was very confusing: two minds, many distractions, powerful self-will, and dread at the thought of sitting in one place for three months having to listen to people talk endlessly about themselves while back home bank loans drained all my reserves.

This is what filled my mind until suddenly one morning in early December, fifteen or twenty miles along the bush road into Camp 23, under a brilliant winter sun high in a cloudless blue sky, I heard a voice that I swear to this day was not my own.

"WHAT IF YOU *DID* TAKE THE DEVELOPMENT COURSE?"

It startled me so much that I almost slid off the icy road trying to stop the truck.

Was it a voice, a presence, or simply an opening in my own mind allowing a new idea to enter? Perhaps it was an interplay of all three. How could I know for sure? I do know that I am a practical person with a well-developed capacity for logic and reason, and what I heard just didn't make sense. The voice was so real I had to stop the truck and get out just to feel the ground.

"What the hell is going on?" I said out loud as my reason began to falter.

Beside me a large clump of snow slid off the branch of a tree by the side of the road. Somewhere deep in the bush a jay's cry pierced the cold stillness. I stopped, shook my head, then turned and started to walk back towards the truck. A wonderful open feeling had come over me, the way a river must feel in spring after breaking through a dam of winter debris. It was my first conscious awareness of something that Swami Radha said to me on our trip when she had first made reference to the possibility of unfinished business.

"Certain things will not be obvious to you," she had said, "because you've already set your mind on something else."

The divine messenger's question had challenged my preconceived ideas about the winter log haul and the yoga course, and helped me to see that the conflict between the two was more imagined than real—a struggle between opposing desires. No matter where it had come from, the question forced me to think about the yoga course, not as a potential intrusion into another desire which I had already set my mind on, but as a unique option having its own special merit. As I approached the landing an idea started to form in my mind.

It seemed that everyone was there before me that morning. By the time I got to the landing there were three trucks ahead of me waiting to be loaded. I sat for a few minutes watching the loader reach over to pick up bunches of spruce and pine logs from a pile by the side of the road and swing them onto the trailer deck of the lead truck. On a good day it would take no more than ten or fifteen minutes to load fifty tons of wood onto one truck. So far it was a very good day. I got out and walked over to the waiting loggers.

"If any of you guys heard about a truck and trailer you could lease for the winter haul," I said, trying to sound indifferent, "what would you do?"

Dennis Johnson didn't hesitate for a second.

"I'd sign right now," he said, and the rest nodded their heads.

Maybe it was the thought of all the money they could make running a couple of extra trucks over winter that made them so agreeable. Whatever it was I got the message and called Dennis that night. And that was how I ended up taking the yoga development course that winter. The ripples of awareness that had been flowing across my mind during the previous weeks had gained enough momentum to push aside my resistance and take me to the next step.

CHAPTER EIGHT

Krishna's Swing

On the second day of Swami Radha's Silver Jubilee celebration in the summer of 1981, I proposed to my family that we move to the ashram to live. Although the heady atmosphere of the celebration marking the twenty-fifth anniversary of her sanyas initiation may have contributed impetus to my proposal, it wasn't based on that alone. Two dreams that summer, and one from the previous fall, all pointed to the same thing: I was living in the ashram, and I had a job of rebuilding to do. Although the dreams were precise, I still needed more time to see clearly what was supposed to be rebuilt. In that summer of 1981, I could only surmise what Swami Radha meant when she described the path of Kundalini yoga as "building the inner Cathedral of Consciousness." Nevertheless, I could hear the conviction in my voice when I stood in front of my wife and daughter that day.

"We are so happy here," I said. "Why would we keep going back and forth across the country if this is where we are meant to be?"

My question unlocked the door. That evening we went to see Swami Radha with our plan. She seemed to know already what was on our minds and was very happy.

"Be here by Christmas," she said. "It's beautiful here at Christmas. We have a great time."

She laughed and hugged us both.

"Donna and David and Alicia are coming to live in the ashram," she told everyone who had come into her sunroom to see what all the excitement was about. "They'll be here by Christmas!"

It was the middle of August. We had only that afternoon made our decision. There was no way we could get here by Christmas. Christmas was only four months away.

"I don't think it's possible, Swami Radha. I've got two trucks to sell and all the equipment that goes with them, and we have to get the money together and everything. No. I'm sure it'll take at least a year to do all that."

"Well," she replied, her voice a little more serious now, "we'll have to see what happens. The major thing is you've decided to come. We should have a little Dubonnet to celebrate."

She turned to one of the swamis in the room and asked him to bring the wine and some glasses.

"And look in the refrigerator to see if there's any almond cake," she called after him.

~

We didn't make it by Christmas, although having the date as our objective gave us the impetus to keep going. Many obstacles arose: unfinished business and a recession in the wood market which made it a bad time to try selling logging equipment, to name only two. And then there were the blockages thrown up by my own self-will trying to make it all happen. The harder I tried the worse it got. Finally after one interminably long frozen night broken down on the highway with a full load and a sheared axle bearing, I quit fighting. The next morning after delivering the load to the mill, I stopped at the truck dealership on my way out of Thunder Bay and went to find one of the salesmen I knew well.

"You see that rig out there?" I said to him. "Well, here's what I need for it."

I wrote the dollar figure down on a piece of paper, handed him the keys, smiled, and walked out of the office and across the yard to the highway heading north to Sioux Lookout. The first truck to come along was going all the way, and that's how I got home. I didn't know enough then to say, "It's all in God's hands," or even to recognize the hand of God when it came along. But that's what began to happen once I acknowledged that I couldn't do it alone.

Christmas, such as it was that year, came and went and winter crawled towards spring with us still clearing up our lives to make the move. Every now and then something would happen to break through the obstacles, as when the salesman called late one afternoon in mid-February to say he had an offer for the truck. It was just enough to pay off the debt and get us to the ashram.

"We'll go soon," I said to Donna. "I have a feeling it won't be long now."

From the time we made our decision to our arrival in the ashram in mid-April of the following year, many lessons involving the interplay of self-will and surrender were learned. Knowing when to act, when to wait and allow a direction to emerge on its own, learning how to be considerate of each other during a time of considerable stress—many times the three of us had to stop and address what was happening between us. When we entered into a contract to keep our divine appointment, all sorts of unexpected things happened—some wonderful, some not so wonderful. The play of opposites that is the basis of all creation became much more apparent after we made our decision, and the obstacles that arose from the play I gradually came to see as the integral challenges of a complex process rather than frustrating blocks to a desired end. Instead of continuing to fight and resist the obstacles, I learned to observe them as reflections of my own mind.

It took us eight months to get to the ashram which was better than the year I had thought we would need. A few days after our arrival, Swami Radha invited us over to Many Mansions for a little welcoming celebration with the other residents. The invitation started me thinking about the extraordinary transition we had gone through as a family over the preceding year, and how much energy had been exhausted just to get here. The hardest part of the move came immediately after I loaded the last of our boxes into the rented truck and locked the cargo door. As I walked up the steps to the front door of our house, it suddenly hit me that in a few minutes I would be pulling out of this driveway for the last time, never to see this place again. The realization shocked me. I sat down on the porch step and looked out over the lake as I had done countless times before, only this time I tried almost desperately to will this precious, beautiful place into a memory I could keep forever. Then suddenly I broke down and sobbed like a child. Finally I understood that it was an essential part of myself that I had met on the shore that day, years ago, a part that somehow I knew must never be forsaken. The North had fulfilled its promise. It was time to take the next step.

"We're lucky to be here even now," I told the group of residents who gathered at Many Mansions to welcome us. "It was quite a job getting it all together and there were many times when I seriously doubted we could make it. But Swami Radha had said be here by Christmas so I always had that somewhere in the back of my mind even though I didn't think we could do it."

Everyone laughed. We all knew from experience that Swami Radha never accepted our self-imposed limitations without challenging the beliefs we used to prop them up.

"It has to do with momentum," she said, looking at me but addressing everyone in the room as well. "You have to think what it has taken just to get you to this point in time. How many lifetimes has it taken just to have the opportunity to try again? We don't know. Perhaps we can never know. Gurudev said that it can take thousands of lifetimes for one who has left the path to have a favorable birth and another chance. But when the decision is made and the momentum has gathered to help it along…well, of course, I would do whatever I could to encourage that. Because, you see, it can't last. The momentum, the force that got you here, is like an ocean wave coming onto the beach with all its power, then receding back into the ocean after the power is spent. That's how it is when you start out on the spiritual path, too. The Divine opens the door creating the opportunity to enter. If you see it and the pressure is there, perhaps from other lifetimes, then you'll go through it. But if you don't the door will close and the opportunity will be lost. It may be a long time before the conditions are right to try again. A very long time. So don't waste this opportunity. Om Om."

Swami Radha pranamed and smiled happily at everyone in the room. These were her close devotees, all gathered together in her house to welcome the new ones to the ashram.

A few weeks later, I stopped by Many Mansions on my way to lunch to deliver a message to her. She surprised me by inviting me to stay and have lunch. I accepted, but I wasn't at all prepared for this unexpected turn. I had been working on the farm all morning and now with her standing right in front of me inviting me to stay, I suddenly became aware of my soiled work clothes clinging to my back in the heat. The dirty jeans and oil-stained shirt were not aspects of myself that I wanted to bring to her table.

We sat together not saying much, taking time to sense each other. I was nervous, wondering what I could possibly say that would be even remotely interesting to one who knew so much about life and who obviously could see further into my mind than I would ever want to. It did not occur to me that she had invited me because she actually wanted me there with her.

"It's funny," she said. "Have you noticed? Even though we don't spend a lot of time together, we seem to take up right from where we left off, as if no time had passed?"

I quickly searched my mind trying to recall the details of the last time I had been with her. Was it yesterday? A week ago? I couldn't recall. As my anxiety increased the point of what she was saying receded further and further from my reasoning powers. It wasn't until I had finished lunch and was walking back along the road to the farm that it hit me.

"My God," I said to myself. "She wasn't talking about last week. She was talking about another time, long ago, long before the memories of this lifetime began."

At Kootenay Bay in spring, the evening sun has to stretch to clear the snow-capped mountain peaks across the lake from the ashram. Kutenai is the name of the people who have lived along the shores of the lake for thousands of years. The word means placid. When I think of Kootenay Lake, though, placidity does not come readily to my mind. The mountains along both shores of the long, narrow lake form a natural funnel that seems to draw the cold wind down from the north. The wind churns the lake into a frenzy and small pleasure boats, caught by surprise, quickly turn to shore. Most make it. A few have not.

Today the lake is calm and reflective and the air is sweet with the fragrance of apple blossoms lingering in the afternoon sun. By early evening the receding light will cast long, serpentine shadows across the ashram and the chill in the air will remind us that winter is still in the mountains above us. As the sun disappears over the jagged peaks, the temple's white dome begins to glow in the soft evening light like a jewel at the heart of Swami Radha's work.

The ashram sits on a ridge of land carved into the side of a gently sloping mountain overlooking Kootenay Lake. Good soil and proximity to the lake made the ridge, which runs several miles along the east shore, a preferred choice of the predominantly British homesteaders who arrived here at the end of the nineteenth century. More than a few of the remaining settlements along the shoreline bear names reminiscent of India under the British Raj.

In 1963, when Swami Radha went to the land registry office across the lake in Kaslo to check the title and confirm the legal description of the property she was considering for the ashram, she was amazed to see that the land had been called "Yasodhara Estates" by its first owner in the late 1800s. Princess Yasodhara, wife of the Buddha, became his first female disciple. Towards the end of her life she started the first Buddhist order for nuns. After pondering this, Swami Radha took it as a sign that women would one day come to the ashram to become strong in the teachings of yoga and eventually carry on her work.

Enter the ashram and you enter your mind. This is the secret. Although it took me many years to discover it, the ashram is a perfect reflection of my mind. I could love it one day and find myself wondering if I could really love anything the next. Reflecting on the play of my emotions over the months prior to moving to the ashram and after my first two years living here, I came to the conclusion that under the sway of emotions nothing is real. With every challenge my emotions created powerful illusions which had no substance to sustain me through the trials. Help could only come after I began to abandon the arrogant notion that I didn't need it.

CHAPTER NINE

Rose Initiation

*We are sitting together by the goldfish pond in Swami Radha's garden
at Many Mansions, on a warm, sunny afternoon in June. It is exactly
two months to the day since Donna and I arrived at the ashram to
begin our two-year residency. This is a magic day, spontaneous, inef-
fable, each part effortlessly dissolving into the next. The bridal wreath
hedge circles the garden like a diadem, its snow-white blossoms show-
ering confetti in the gentle breeze. Nothing is fixed; at times it feels as
if we are sitting in the center of a floating garden, carried by the soft
undulating waves beneath us. Do I understand what is happening?
Not really, not consciously anyway. It seems clear that the Rose Ceremony Swami Radha is offering us is meant to acknowledge both our
marriage and our spiritual aspirations—and remind us that the one
commitment is not exclusive of the other.*

I knew something important was being initiated though I couldn't
find the words to explain it even to myself. Yet the setting seemed so
natural and familiar—the three of us sitting together on a blanket laid
out on the lawn in her garden, between the hedge and a small magno-
lia tree. As Swami Radha talked, I imagined that we were being held in
a triangle of Light.

"I have a special gift for you," she said, picking up a small pewter
box. "I want you to take great care of it and one day, when you're ready
and we've agreed, you can bring it back—in six months, a year, two
years. In the meantime take great care of it."

She opened the box and took out three tiny envelopes.

"This is holy ash from India," she said, carefully opening the first envelope. "And this is some of the rice that my guru gave to me," she said, giving us each a few grains from the second envelope. "And the red powder you use to mark the space between your eyebrows, where you focus in your meditation."

Here she took a tiny smudge of the powder from the third envelope and touched our foreheads.

"I want you both to take great care of these things," she said, putting them carefully back into the box. "Now, Donna, you come and sit here."

Swami Radha took a white cotton shawl from around her shoulders and motioned for Donna to come close. Then she reached out and wrapped the shawl around Donna's shoulders.

"At night you can fold it up and put it on your pillow, and that will help you to keep meditating while you are asleep," she said, looking with great warmth into Donna's eyes.

Then she turned to me.

"I hope I've made it big enough."

She laughed as she took a second shawl and placed it around my shoulders. We hugged.

"At some point," she continued, "we can have a spiritual marriage ceremony if you like, but in its own time. Everything has its own time and we are in no hurry for this. We would also need to talk about what spiritual marriage means. But this is the first step you are taking today, so...and then we'll take another step, and when the time is ready we can take another step, and after that a few more. But it's up to you. You decide how many lifetimes you want to take."

I flashed to yesterday and our offering of the rose petals that represented the pairs of opposites in each of us*. One by one we placed the petals into the crystal bowl of water, and with each offering requested

*See Swami Sivananda Radha, The Rose Ceremony (Spokane: Timeless Books, 1997).

Divine Love in return—pain and love; anger and compassion; selfishness and gratitude—all the opposites that created the illusion of separation, each offered symbolically while asking for Divine Love in return. For Donna and me, the Rose Ceremony celebrated the ideal of union in our marriage while taking that ideal to another level of meaning—our individual union with the Most High. That night, Swami Radha asked each of us to make a list of our grudges and resentments for burning the next day. After I made my list, I put it in an envelope, sealed it, and wrote my name on the outside. When it came time to burn the list I put the whole envelope unopened into the fire. Swami Radha had been sitting by the fire watching us both intently.

"Do you see what you did?" she asked.

I nodded as I watched the flames start to curl and blacken the edges of the envelope.

"Do you know why? Was it intentional or unconscious?"

"I would have to say it was unconscious."

"So what did your unconscious say?"

"Well, one possibility is that the 'David' associated with those grudges is going to be replaced by someone else."

"Yes, that's a possibility. Everything happens by divine appointment, I've seen that over and over. And sometimes these things can only come to you in a state of mind that is somewhere between dreaming and waking. It would be good to observe your dreams, particularly any recent ones, to see if there were any signs pointing in this direction. How old are you?"

"Thirty-eight."

"Umm…well, it has taken all those years to nourish the ego. Don't think that in a few weeks or a few months you can diminish it. You have to build a spiritual bank account and even after the first half-million you don't stop worrying, right? You keep building your spiritual bank account until you have a hundred thousand mantras in there and you know it's okay. That's where you'll find your security. Nowhere else."

That was in the morning. Now in the afternoon, in her garden, we were taking the next step. I still didn't understand what it was all about except that it felt as though we were forging a very special relationship. The atmosphere was sublime, like a wedding almost. Swami Radha continued, her voice soft and relaxed.

"The shawls came from some kind of prompting. In fact nothing we've done here was figured out beforehand. If you allow yourself to follow such inner prompting and record what happens in your diary as a result, then you will always have some way to see the Light even when the clouds are overhead. You can look at the clouds and say to them, 'Well, you haven't always been there and you will go again, so I don't have to give you the importance you demand.' In other words, you don't give the clouds the power to stay. You can find the same idea in the New Testament where Jesus warned us not to fight evil because it has the power to draw us in and we can end up being controlled by it. There is so much more evil than your tiny little spiritual self can stand, so it's important not to get involved in the first place. This doesn't mean you're a coward or that you're not concerned. It just means seeing the facts for what they are."

Swami Radha turned to watch a robin fly to her nest on the stone wall by the fish pond.

"The mind can be like a monster," she said, as we watched the robin feeding her young. "You stuff something in and the mouth stays wide open. And it's a never-ending process. No, don't even try to satisfy the greedy intellect. The intellect is what keeps you apart. Once the mind gets heavy the body gets heavy. When that happens you're bound to the earth and you'll not recover your celestial body. So shift your gaze instead, and in the meantime build your spiritual bank account. That's where you'll find your security when you need it.

"I'm not sure how strong your Christian upbringing was," she said, looking at me, "but if it's in you then you must make the effort to study some of the doctrine yourself. You'll see that there is nothing in the church that had not already been in existence in the East for at least a couple of thousand years before Christ. The cross, the Eucharist, the pope, they all have their counterpart in the East. The similarity between the mala and the rosary is just one example. So you don't have to be intimidated by what we're doing here. It's not so unique.

"I say this because things will happen on the spiritual path. You both have already encountered lots of obstacles in getting here; in fact, I would have questioned it if you had been able to come here in one smooth sailing. If it had worked that way you could just as smoothly sail out when the tests come. The tests you encounter on the path are not for the gods or for the ashram or for me. They are for you to know where you are, where you stand."

Swami Radha looked around the garden at the flowering bushes and smiled.

"The blossoms this year are the nicest we've ever had! Can you take a picture? The white will show against the white. So! Be happy! Be happy in your heart."

The laburnum tree next to the goldfish pond was in full bloom, its golden yellow blossoms translucent in the afternoon sun. We all got up from the blanket and Swami Radha moved to a garden chair placed beside the tree for the photo session. As she sat down, the blossoms cascaded around her in a shower of golden sunlight. It is a scene I often recall in difficult and challenging times and each time it sustains me, reminding me again of the powerful conviction that has brought me back to my spiritual home.

CHAPTER TEN

Entering

I had been at the ashram for less than six months when Swami Radha called me from the home of one of her students in Redwood City, near San Francisco. She had spent most of the summer in Redwood City, using the available time and solitude to work on a new manuscript. She had also been meeting with Michael and Justine Toms, founders of the fledgling New Dimensions Radio Network in San Francisco, and had already done a couple of interviews with Michael when she called. She told me that she had found him to be a particularly sensitive and intelligent interviewer. "He knows how to listen," she said. Now Michael and Justine were exploring the idea of inviting Swami Radha to form a partnership with them in a kind of spiritual advisory capacity. Because of my background in radio, Swami Radha was calling to see if I could meet with them, too.

"You can just be here," she said. "Tape record the meeting, listen to their proposal and take notes, and see what you think."

I immediately said yes, and made arrangements that afternoon to get myself to San Francisco.

On the morning we drove into San Francisco for our meeting, Swami Radha explained how she entered new situations with people. She stressed the importance of getting involved in a way that was courteous to the Toms while applying the principle as I would to any new experience. By principle, I think she meant the Light. She said it was important for me to understand that they had been doing something for quite awhile without me, and that it was a privilege to be of service to them.

"Learn to see everyone and every event as a divine opportunity," she said. "If we are going to work together I approach on their terms, in their style, until we have some experience of each other and have gained a little trust. Then when problems come up, an opportunity to be of help from my personal experience exists because the groundwork has been done and my suggestions can be received in the manner in which they have been presented. Again, it is a delicate balance."

We found a parking place on States Street just a few doors from the pale clapboard house that had been converted into a studio and office for New Dimensions Radio. As we walked up the steps to the front door, the thought came to me that this time with Swami Radha was a wonderful opportunity coming to me early in our relationship. I was deeply grateful to be with her. I would often see her in Light—almost a translucent whiteness—and lately I had become aware of how deep my feelings for her could be at these times. I felt she was truly my spiritual mother and my love for her was starting to deepen into feelings of gratitude that surprised me with their intensity. But they confused me as well. My work with Swami Radha's teachings had revealed many different aspects of my male self, some very positive and useful, others not so positive. But when it came to finer feelings, I was unsure. Where were they taking me? Where did they come from? I had learned to hide such sensitivity well, but in her company that sensitivity would sometimes come back to me in waves that were almost overwhelming.

In those early days with Swami Radha it was not unusual for me to go back and forth between feelings of deep gratitude and real fear that I would somehow lose control if I allowed myself to get too close to her. Then an old familiar personality would come into play, a kind of easygoing take-it-for-granted character whose relaxed disposition and casual speech masked a powerful need for control. My notes from the morning after our meeting with the Toms reminded me again of how this personality would play out, almost as a foil to deflect my finer feelings.

ENTERING 87

I know a little bit more about surrender this morning. Just before bedtime last night, Swami Radha called me into her study for a visit. "Great!" I said. "Just let me get some coffee and I'll be right with you." When I came back to her room a few minutes later she had gone to take a shower. I sat and waited for her to come back and wondered at the arrogance of my assumptions. Surrender and service do not require a coffee first, I thought. At least she is making good use of the delay I have inflicted upon her.

Swami Radha and I met with the Toms for lunch the next day and by the end of the week we were on our way home from San Francisco, driving together back to the ashram. She had given me the tape to transcribe from our first meeting but had said no more about what the next step might be. That was fine with me. I had enjoyed meeting the Toms but I didn't feel I knew enough about Swami Radha's work to offer much in the way of advice. As far as radio was concerned it was clear to me they knew what they were doing.

After two days on the road with her, I felt calm, peaceful and clear in my speech and my thinking. The challenge for me was to sustain that clarity back in the ashram. The thing was not to get caught in the ashram as a physical place but to remember that my purpose here was spiritual growth, first and foremost, and the work here and the interactions with people were the means for that to happen. It was clear to me that detachment was essential in order to remain straight, clear, and honest with everyone, most of all myself. For me this meant devotional practice and careful observance of my speech at all times.

My trip to San Francisco had another purpose which only started to become apparent after we got back to the ashram. Swami Radha asked me to bring the transcription of our meeting with the Toms over to Many Mansions when I finished it so that we could discuss it together. That night I started transcribing the tape after my regular work on the farm. It seemed to go fine except that I began to feel unusually tired after an hour or so of listening and typing. Must be the farm work, I thought, and went to bed early. But the next night the same thing happened, and again the night after that. By the time I finished transcribing the tape, I was feeling so tired and heavy that I thought I must be coming down with something. The only inconsistency was that I had lots of energy and vigor during the day. I puzzled about this on my way over to Many Mansions with the finished transcript. It was not like me to feel so tired and weighted down, particularly since coming to live in the ashram.

We sat together in the sunroom while I read the transcript out loud. Afterwards I told her about the curious physical response I'd had while typing it. She gave me one of her searching looks. Then without saying a word she put her copy of the transcript down on the desk and looked out the window across the lake, far away, absorbed in thoughts I could not even guess at. I waited.

"How is your work going on the farm?" she asked.

"Good. I'm liking it a lot."

"Hmm...and Ron? You are getting along all right with him?"

"Very well. I like him very much. We work well together."

"Good. That is always a great help to me when people in the ashram are able to work together harmoniously. When that harmony isn't there, it is a very great strain on me, I can assure you."

I smiled and waited, relieved to hear that what I was doing was a help to her. But I was having trouble understanding why our meeting was taking this particular direction. Had I said something? Done something wrong? Why was she no longer interested in the San Francisco project? What had she seen?

Suddenly she smiled at me and said gently, "This is your place, David. Do you know that? This is your place."

I nodded, unable to speak. The intense truth of what she had said needed time to be absorbed. After a few minutes of sitting quietly, a great weight seemed to lift from my mind and a deep feeling of relief spread all through my chest and shoulders as I let myself sink into her care. It was no longer necessary for me to know what she had seen when I described my reaction to the transcript. It was enough just to experience freedom from the judgment and condemnation that had hounded me most of my life, and to recognize that she was seeing in me something much greater, a consciousness perhaps, that went far beyond the day-to-day David who survived by his instincts and his intellect.

CHAPTER ELEVEN

Marriage, Family, and Spiritual Life

N ine months after moving to the ashram, I wrote a paper called *Marriage and Spiritual Life at the Ashram—an Update*. Fifteen years later, going through my diary notes for this book, I came across a reference to this paper. I dug it out of my files and was immediately struck by the bland formality of the title. Like a quarterly business report, it revealed nothing of the emotional after-effects of a major strategic decision. Given the extent to which we had turned our lives upside down, emotions had to have been a larger part of the process than the title suggests.

Reading the paper again certainly confirmed this. But with the hindsight afforded by time, I could also see the clarity of the thoughts that were in my subconscious at the time. I wrote the paper in the midst of a struggle between my two minds: the emotional mind that hung onto the family as an illusory embodiment of love and the aspiring mind which sought to fulfill its spiritual ideals. Each seemed to have a power of its own and clearly they were not reconciled to each other.

I've heard new mothers say that pregnancy, as sublime as it can be at times, is not without pain and confusion as well. I think the same can be said for bringing a spiritual baby into the world. In my own case, attachment on the one hand and a powerful desire for personal liberation on the other created a polarity of cross-purposes that often created pain and confusion for all of us. A fact of spiritual life is that it calls for the eventual renunciation of attachments. When we made our decision to move to the ashram, we both knew that we were embarking on a path that was destined to change our marriage, possibly in quite dramatic ways. The paper made it clear that it was time to get on with the job I had come to do. Here is part of what I wrote.

> *During the past few weeks I have become uncertain about how to live a married life while trying to give attention to my purpose for being here. When I first came to live in the ashram, I resolved to fulfill three goals in the first year. The first was to finish my book reports,* the second was to serve the ashram in whatever capacity I was asked to serve with as much good will as I could bring to the task. The third was to bring a stronger sense of devotion into my life. As I work towards these goals, I find that my overall attitude towards a number of things has changed in the process. In work, I have much more energy available for the task and far less fear concerning the outcome. It is a pleasure for me to work in the ashram, an attitude that seems connected to the fact that I am much more consistent in my prayer and in my use of the Divine Light Invocation.** Regular attendance at satsang has helped considerably.*
>
> *In spite of all this, my concentration and consistency are threatened by sentimentality. The ashram is a very busy place and here there are plenty of distractions that lead me away from my first-year goals. Awareness of this has challenged my willingness to sustain a marriage in the ashram while so many other areas of my spiritual development are calling for my attention.*

---

* A requirement of the three-month Yoga Development Course.

** See Swami Sivananda Radha, *The Divine Light Invocation* (Spokane: Timeless Books, 1990) or Swami Sivananda Radha, *Kundalini Yoga for the West* (Spokane: Timeless Books, 1993). The Divine Light Invocation is a spiritual practice which, when diligently practiced, enables the student to identify with the Light.

My paper on marriage seemed oddly distant from the passions that had fueled our desire to live together. I say oddly because I never expected those passions to subside. Neither of us knew anything about the ashram when we first married, which is probably just as well. I doubt that we would have had much inclination to reflect on the spiritual implications of our union, so absorbed were we in each other at the time.

Considering how we began it's amazing we got together at all. If it hadn't been for the bible on the back seat of Donna's car, I might just as easily have dismissed our chance encounter as a purely circumstantial coming together of two people who otherwise would have remained strangers to each other. But the bible changed all that. A few days after I returned to work, I came back from lunch one afternoon and found a new copy of the *Jerusalem Bible* sitting on my desk with a thank-you card from Donna and Alicia tucked inside.

That must be where it started for us. The gift touched me deeply, but it brought up confusion as well. On my vacation, I had stopped by to see a network producer in Toronto, who promptly offered me a job on a new show starting that fall. She was eager to have me start a month before the beginning of the fall program season, which meant in her parlance, Get here as soon as you can! I was ready to inform the people I worked with in Thunder Bay, but now all these unexpected feelings were coming up in me around a woman I hardly knew. Besides, she already had a daughter and maybe the whole thing was just my imagination anyway, and probably the best thing for me to do was to keep moving, keep my focus on the job ahead. So that's how I managed to override my heart. I steeled my resolve, gave notice, and started packing, all of which did absolutely nothing to alter what was happening between us.

"I would like to keep your friendship," she said. "Friendship is very important to me and so I work at it."

I didn't say anything, waiting to be certain I'd heard right. After all, it was late—two in the morning—and nothing can be as it appears or sounds at this hour. There we were sitting on the front porch of her house, and against all reason I had drawn close to her, like a bee hovering over a blossom, drawn by the alluring color and sweet scent. But here the story becomes confounded by a harsh reality. As I sat staring into the darkness, it came to me again that I would soon be leaving to start my new job in another city far away. How do I say goodbye to a new friend who most likely I shall never see again? At two in the morning this struck me as grievously unfair, a matter of dreadful timing, and I was almost overwhelmed with the sad realization that something extremely precious was about to be lost again, and I was helpless to prevent it from happening.

"But that's why I'm telling you this," she said, as her hand brushed against mine. "Just because you're going away doesn't mean the end of our friendship."

And that's how immaculate reasoning kept us together. A week later I moved into an old brick house on a quiet street in downtown Toronto. Two months after that Donna and Alicia moved in with me and, with the exception of one unforeseen and entirely unexpected item, it was all coming together better than I had ever dreamed possible. Lynne Waboose was the unexpected item.

Lynne Waboose. She was a spunky, eight-year-old Cree from northern Ontario, slightly undersized for her age, but sturdy and determined, nevertheless. Lynne had the muscular, slightly bowed gait of one born to grow up on the gravel roads and bush paths of an isolated northern village. Yet there was one major discrepancy. As a long-term ward of Children's Aid, Lynne had been in and out of southern foster homes most of her life. Her way of surviving was to see her keepers as an endless source of amusement. A perpetual, faintly sardonic grin masked the pain inside her. By the time I met her she had gone through enough foster homes to have developed a chameleon-like adaptability to the world. We had agreed to look after her temporarily to help a friend of Donna's, a Children's Aid worker who had run out of options. What I didn't realize when I first met Lynne, standing beside Alicia in the hallway of our house in Toronto, was that she was a divine messenger—

she, and the woman who sat across from me at the dinner party organ-
ized a few days later by a friend to welcome us back to the city.

It was somewhere between the first and second course, in the
middle of a story I was relating about my new family status, that the
woman suddenly exclaimed in a furious, ringing voice, "I have never
heard anything so pompous and ridiculous in my life."

She was referring to something I had just said. A hush immediately
descended over the soup. I wondered, Shall I create a scene or just
leave? I turned to my hosts for relief from this acutely embarrassing
situation and was shocked to see their obvious delight at this sudden
effusion of feminine indignation at their dinner table. I began to consider the possibility that perhaps I had said something dumb. Dumb,
and as with all speech, revealing as well.

Lynne, the messenger, had started it all by calling me "Daddy" within
the first three minutes of her arrival at my door.

"Hey, Daddy," she said. "You goin' out, eh?"

Alicia stood beside her in the hallway looking at me wide-eyed, not
saying a word. Two little girls, almost identical in size, one a gutsy,
brown-skinned Cree with shiny black bangs and slightly bowed legs;
the other, half her age with honey-blonde hair, fair skin, and deep blue
eyes reflecting a cautious reserve. A palpable irony had already made
them inseparable. Lynne had learned to survive in alien territory: the
foster homes of white people in the south. Alicia had spent the first
two years of her life in Big Trout Lake, a Cree village north of Sioux
Lookout. Her first spoken words were Cree—the language of the children who played with her every day. And now here they were, the two
of them in my house in Toronto, and somehow I was supposed to be
their daddy. I didn't know what to say.

Lynne asked me again.

"Hey, Daddy. You goin' somewhere, eh?"

I looked down at the cheeky grin and beaming face and realized
that wherever I was going, it would not be alone. Two days of "Hey
Daddy" and Alicia came to me one morning, very tentative, and asked

if she could call me "Daddy" too. Till the day I die, I shall never forget the sight of her standing in front of me waiting while I stumbled around in near panic trying to avoid the question.

Mustering all of my moral reserves into the quiet, steady voice of reason I said, "Well, I don't think that would be right. I don't want to be the cause of any confusion between you and your father."

That's what I said, but even as I heard the words I knew they were nothing but empty platitudes. Her father left soon after she was born and had made almost no contact since. The truth was that "yes" implied a commitment that I was not ready to make. There was no way I could take on that kind of responsibility so fast, which is how I explained it to everyone, including the single mother of three young children sitting across from me that night at the dinner party. But she had seen too much of the male world, too much of the arrogance and insensitivity behind my words. So she challenged them.

The next morning, I took Alicia onto my knee and told her she could call me Daddy any time. In fact she could call me anything she liked.

You can see why Swami Radha's question about "Daddy" touched me so deeply on that first day I met her. That, and the question of "unfinished business" that she brought up on our road trip to Sioux Lookout. If I allow myself to use her questions and comments as catalysts for a deeper inquiry into my experience, then I have nowhere else to go with that experience but to a larger purpose. That is what gives my life meaning, and at times a depth of gratitude for the gift of this life that is beyond description.

Swami Radha often used the analogy of the drop returning to the deep to describe the journey of individual consciousness towards Cosmic Consciousness. Although the metaphor is poetic, her description bridges to a basic, fundamental fact of life: in birth, death is hidden. All that is born, whether it be a thought, a word, an inspiration, a prayer, or another human being, has its own predetermined purpose and allotted time. Once that purpose is fulfilled, the vehicle that was needed to carry out that purpose is no longer of any use. The form dies, transforming itself into a new form and another opportunity. The form changes; the essence does not. Life then can be understood as a preparation for death, and a wise person will use the opportunity to the fullest, not wasting time in an endless repetition of painful illusions. Over my years with Swami Radha's teachings, I have come to understand that my own life with its particular set of circumstances taken as a whole presents an extraordinary opportunity for evolving into Awareness. When I entered her field of Light, I took the first step towards a more conscious cooperation with that evolution.

CHAPTER TWELVE

Fathers and Daughters

One day early in July, just three months after moving to the
ashram, I spent the morning scything grass in a field below
the orchard. The grass was almost up to my waist, I had my
shirt off, and it was hard going.

Swish, swish, balance, rhythm…
rotate the body
through the hips…
don't just swing
the arms…
let the scythe do the work.

I kept repeating the instructions I'd heard earlier that morning, struggling to find that elusive place of synchronicity where the scythe and I
would become one. I stopped, wiped the sweat out of my eyes, and
muttered something unrepeatable. Suddenly I heard Swami Radha's
cheerful greeting behind me.

"Ah! Swami Radha. Hello. Yes. Um…. How are you?"

My voice boomed across the short distance between us, while inside another voice urged me to calm down. I was always happy to see
her, though she seemed to have a perfect knack for appearing at the
most inopportune time. Dirty, sweaty, greasy hands, oil-stained cover-
alls, machinery, tools, engines, bits and pieces all over the shop floor,

shirt lying in the grass nearby, taking a smoke break, it all added up to one thing: my mind was a poor receiving line for such a refined lady.

She often said that if you focus on the Light in a person you'll see the Light instead of the ever-performing personality aspects. Image and self-image. What does my mind project onto another? I could see that her focus on the Light would be a protection for both of us.

Today in the field it was Alicia that was on her mind. She asked me what my plans were for her education. Had I thought about her schooling now that we were living as a family in the ashram? I told her that apart from setting aside enough money to get Alicia through high school and into university, I had not thought much about the actual form that schooling would take. Alicia seemed happy enough to be going to the local public school and I had seen no reason to consider other options for the fall. Besides she was just twelve years old and thoughts about her leaving home to go away to school had never entered my mind. But they were starting to now.

"There are excellent schools in Switzerland," she said. "I may have someone there who could find the right school."

I must have looked dumbfounded because I knew we didn't have anywhere near enough money for that kind of schooling. Besides, how could I even begin to think about Alicia leaving home at just twelve, let alone going to school halfway around the world? Swami Radha nodded, smiled, and told me the story of a family who had sent their daughter to a good school in Europe.

"It gave her a perspective she would otherwise never have had," she said. "The daughter learned how to converse, how to fit into different social circumstances. She saw a whole world apart from the limited viewpoint of her upbringing, and that gave her confidence. A young woman needs that confidence."

Swami Radha smiled at me and turned to go. Then she paused.

"When Alicia turns seventeen or eighteen," she said, "buy her something special and take her out to a very good restaurant for dinner. In this way you will give her the message that she is precious in your eyes.

You are the first man in her life and how you treat her will determine how she will let herself be treated by other men in the future."

All this while standing in the field of tall grass, just the two of us under the morning sun, while I tried to keep trusting, tried to remain open to the unthinkable. But it was hard. I just couldn't bring myself to the idea of sending my daughter away. I looked at the grass waving in the gentle breeze and watched the sunlight break into a million radiant particles on the surface of the lake. In spite of the early summer heat, little patches of snow clung to the mountain peaks on the far shore, like sun dishes projecting the light back to its source. What will my daughter see in the future? What will she need to survive in the world? She did not choose to live in an ashram in the mountains of British Columbia. Her parents made that choice. What is our responsibility to her?

The guru looks over the field gathering facts. Some weeds here, good grass over there, wildflowers in abundance. Judging by the healthy growth the soil appears to be good. Cultivate the ground, lay the foundation, plant the seed, see what happens, be patient enough to allow the unseen to come into manifest form in its own time. It takes nine months for the baby to be born. Why do I think renunciation should happen overnight? Why do I think renunciation should happen at all? Am I only a temporary caretaker for this little soul? These thoughts go very deep. The seed has all the potential needed for a lifetime. The seed has been planted and awaits its time.

That night Swami Radha invited Donna and me to visit her in her sunroom after satsang. She was welcoming and friendly.

"Both of you must understand," she said. "I was simply opening up the options for you to think about the little girl's future. I am not saying that she has to go away from the ashram. You must understand that."

We did, but it was still a relief to hear her say it. I could feel the idea receding into the background and my image of family returning to normal. It was ironic in a way. Nothing we were doing as a family even approached the normal, yet I clung to the illusion for the security it provided. Swami Radha understood this. In all my years I never once saw her take anything from anyone without having something far more substantial to put in its place.

Two years later on a Sunday evening in late June, Alicia and I were on our way to the barn to milk the cows. The air was mild, warm from the heat of the day, and the light from the setting sun cast soft shadows across the garden and through the trees. Alicia was just home from a weekend horse show in a nearby town where she had won every class and had placed first overall in her age group. She was silent as we walked towards the barn and I sensed that something in her wasn't quite settled from the weekend.

"You seem pretty quiet for someone who has taken top honors in everything she did."

"Yes."

"So maybe winning wasn't such a big deal?"

"No."

"Can you say why?"

"Well, there wasn't any challenge. I've competed against the same people for years and it wasn't that hard to do well."

"Ah."

I could hear it in her voice—she was puzzled but also intrigued by this unusual feeling of ambiguity in the face of winning. I felt she was on the edge of something important. A few more steps along the road together in silence.

"Dad?"

"Yes?"

"I think I would like to go away to school next fall. Could I go to a city?"

She was fourteen. The time had come for her to go into the world and begin to find her own way. Because of a little talk under the summer sun two years earlier, I was prepared and willing to support the next step.

"My father always supported my interest in writing," Swami Radha said, "even before I knew how to write the words."

She laughed as she recalled the first story she'd "written" at the age of three and how kindly her father had received her page of illegible scrawls.

She had been writing her story on the floor in her father's study one afternoon when she heard him come into the house. She jumped up and ran into the vestibule to greet him.

"Would you like to read a story I've written for you? It is about a little girl, and there is something to make you laugh and something to make you cry."

Her father looked at the crumpled sheet of paper clutched in his little daughter's hand.

"Yes, I would be most happy to read it," he replied. Then patting his breast pocket, he added, "But I seem to have misplaced my glasses. Would you read it to me instead?"

She needed no further prompting and proceeded to tell him the whole story, taking great care to include every detail. Of course, her father had known that she could not yet read or write, but he understood the spirit behind her eager anticipation and without missing a beat had entered into it. By the time she was sent to boarding school at the age of eleven, she was quite an accomplished writer. Years later, when she was applying for the job at the Berlin newspaper, her father told her, "You already had the recipe for writing very early in your life. Keep that recipe and you'll do fine."

Swami Radha described her father as her first guru. Although he was in many ways typical of a successful, upper-class continental man, one who moved easily in the salons and mercantile offices of Europe and the Far East, he was unusual in his willingness to take an active interest in preparing his daughter for life, a role usually assigned to the mother or, as was the case in many wealthy houses at the turn of the century, to the nanny or child's nurse. His daughter was precious to him. He respected her intelligence, which is especially important to a small child when such respect can have a profound impact. He had the wisdom to start teaching her the practical facts of life when she was very young and most impressionable, using the immediacy of day-to-day life in their household as his curriculum. He was patient, always taking the time to appeal to her practicality and common sense, and over the years their relationship deepened through the respect they had for each other. Much to the annoyance of her mother, the two spent many hours talking together. They were, first and always, friends, and it was this relationship with her father that established Swami Radha's lifelong standards for true friendship, particularly in relation to men.

One time when she was very young, they were sitting together in his study when her father casually reached down and scratched the ears of one of the two sleeping dogs lying at his feet. Immediately the second dog sprang up, growling at the first one, trying to push it away to get the attention for itself. Her father turned to his daughter and looked closely at her.

"Did you see that?" he asked. "It's jealousy. That's what jealousy is—wanting what the other has. Never, ever lower yourself to the level of a dog, Sylvia, just to get what you think you need. It's not worth it."

Her father did something that very few human fathers seem willing to do: he took the time to teach her about the mating game—sex and the veiled, and not-so-veiled, nuances of seduction and conquest. In the politically ambiguous, nihilistic Berlin of the 1920s, there was no shortage of examples for her to learn from. The problem was to find a way to teach his daughter that would affirm her own intelligence and self-respect. Swami Radha's eyes sparkled as she described his inspired solution.

"When I turned eighteen my father gave me a present of a beautiful evening gown," she said, clearly relishing the memory. "He asked me if I liked it; of course it was wonderful. Then he said, 'Would you like to go out to a nightclub?' A nightclub! And in Germany at that time, the entertainment in a nightclub didn't really start until eleven p.m. or even later! So we went, arriving a little before eleven. I had never been to a nightclub in my life and the first thing I saw was the bar. I wanted to sit there so that I could look around and see everything but my father said, 'No, ladies do not sit at the bar.' He said we would choose a table from which I could see everything.

"So we sat down at a table and I looked around at the other people. I noticed two men sitting at the bar. Another man came in with two women, one with black hair and the other blonde, and the three of them went together to the bar and ordered drinks. Then I heard the two men talking about the women. One of the men described the woman with black hair as looking like a real ball of fire, but was actually quite boring. The blonde one, on the other hand, was supposed to be quite something. I asked my father what they were talking about because it didn't make any sense to me, and he told me outright. Sex. This was a real eye-opener for me.

"I also noticed that my father was smoking one cigarette after another, taking just two or three puffs from each, then stubbing the cigarette out. When I asked him why he was doing that he said, 'Oh, you know, I like to have a change, something different.' But of course he was showing me how the men were treating the women—using them once or twice and then throwing them out. I wondered how many women a man like that could have and my father said, 'Well, there are three hundred and sixty-five days in the year and maybe over two or three years that could add up to five hundred women or more.' I could scarcely believe what I had heard. But I did remember.

"Some time later when the first young man came to our house to ask me out, my answer was, 'No thank you. I don't want to be number five hundred and one.' Of course he didn't know what I was talking about. But I knew. Because of what my father had shown me, I never ever could be used by a man. Many men tried, especially in the photography work and the theater, but to no avail. My father had shown me that in his eyes I was precious, and that was a very important message to me."

I finished jotting down some key words to help me remember the story, then asked Swami Radha how we as parents could talk to our own children about men and women and the mating game. She replied to my question by reminding me of my own experience. We have a duty to tell our children the truth about marriage as we've experienced it, she said, but also to tell them something of what our lives had been before we married. She felt strongly that it was a case of relying on our own experience and being truthful about it, rather than recycling old illusions that would only create more pain.

"Tell your children, when they are attracted to another, that they can keep perspective by remembering that they are considering a friendship. They can ask themselves, Am I prepared to be friends with this person for a long time, or would I even want this person for a friend? If men and women can come together first as friends, then they have a much better chance of staying together over a longer period of time. But it is also important for the young ones to see the mating game as it is. Parents can help prepare their children by being as honest as they can be about their own experience.

"As a man," she said, turning squarely towards me, "you can tell your daughter that her mother was not the first woman you have known, nor are you the first man her mother has known. Tell her, too, that your marriage might not have lasted were it not for the workshop you and Donna took many years ago that helped you through the difficult times. These are the facts about love and marriage. Help them to see the facts as they are."

CHAPTER THIRTEEN

Can you Listen
to a Woman?

T he ashram wasn't always as beautiful and refined as it is today.
When Swami Radha first saw the land in the fall of 1963 it had
already been abandoned for seven years. Tall, coarse grass
reached into the lower branches of the fruit trees that had been planted
in the early part of the century along the road running through the
middle of the property. Left untended, the trees no longer produced as
they once had, though some of the apple trees had large red fruit hanging from the upper branches. Mr. Fraser, a homesteader from the next
valley who had come to show her the property, said they were still on
the tree because they were just out of reach of bears. Many bears forage
through here every spring and fall, he told her.

As with most families over time, the one that had homesteaded this
land for over forty years had gradually dispersed. The house was now
taken over by packrats, mice, chipmunks, and various other critters.
The children who had received much of their schooling in that house
had left to go to university in cities far removed from wilderness life.
Perhaps to be expected, the cities laid claim to them. When their parents finally reached the age where they could no longer manage the
property on their own, they too moved to town. All this happened in
the mid-fifties, around the time Swami Radha was leaving Montreal to
go to India. There was no market for the property then, so the family
simply abandoned it.

Nature had wasted little time reclaiming the empty homestead. By the time Swami Radha arrived, all kinds of creatures had taken up residency in the buildings, the well had filled in, the woodshed roof had collapsed, and these were just some of the more obvious indicators of the immense amount of work that would be needed to make the place habitable again. Nevertheless, one walk over the land with a couple of the young men from the Vancouver Ashram, and they all agreed—this was the place for the new ashram. Swami Radha made a small down payment to hold the property and started to make plans for the move from Vancouver.

Of necessity the ashram facilities remained primitive for the first few years. There was little money and more than enough work just to clean up the property, cut the grass, prune back the fruit trees, and make the buildings usable once again. In one of the back rooms of the main house, Swami Radha found an old French provincial bedroom suite that had become home to an extended family of squirrels. Its chest of drawers was a veritable rodent condominium. Swami Radha encouraged the tenants to leave and began to restore the furniture herself. A friend showed her how to apply an antique finish to the sanded wood and within a few days she had an attractive "new" bedroom suite that she used all the years she lived in the ashram.

Swami Radha's house, Many Mansions, was built for her in 1969 on a prominent rock ledge near the center of the ashram overlooking Kootenay Lake. The modest, split-level ranch-style bungalow would hardly warrant a second glance if you happened to drive by it in any suburb in North America, yet it is a very special house. Many Mansions was Swami Radha's home for almost thirty years. Even today, as I approach the front door of Many Mansions, it is not without memory of the many times I came along this same walk on my way to visit her in the sunroom or to attend the Kundalini class she held for the new residents every Tuesday night during the first two years I lived here. There was always something happening when Swami Radha was living in the house and the rooms vibrated with her vitality. They still do, which from time to time leads me to think that she is never very far away.

On the same promontory of rock next to Many Mansions, the beautiful white-domed Temple of Divine Light was built in 1989. It, too, commands a sweeping panorama of Kootenay Lake. Across the road from the temple is the ashram's farm, which includes a large organic garden and orchard. At the north end of the property above the orchard, you can see the barn where the cows and chickens live. By some quirk of fortune they have the most commanding view of the temple site in the ashram. In 1963, though, all they would have commanded was a view of dense forest and scrub bush, for that was what covered the land now occupied by the Temple, Many Mansions and the garden. Even the craggy knoll that is the site of the present barn was covered in sparse fir and cedar clinging tenaciously to its rock face.

I started working on the farm soon after moving to the ashram, and managed it for seven years—the length of time it took to wear down some of my rougher edges. Just how rough were these edges became apparent early in my career when the issue of the manure spreader suddenly popped up in Swami Radha's sunroom. As I was about to find out, Krishna—beloved of Radha—would use anything, even a manure spreader, to challenge a devotee's arrogance and self-importance.

It was, I have to admit, a remarkably original play. I was at Many Mansions visiting Swami Radha in her sunroom one Saturday afternoon when the intercom buzzed. Swami Radha picked up the phone, listened for a moment, then handed me the receiver. I wondered what phone call could be so important that the office would interrupt Swami Radha in her private quarters. I took the receiver.

"Hello?"

"You the fella lookin' for a manure spreader?" The voice boomed across the line.

"Um...well, uh...yes, as a matter of fact I am, but, uh...."

"Great! I got a real beaut here for ya, and it's only fifteen hundred bucks."

Oh man, I thought. I don't want to go into this now, here of all places. I know I've been looking for a decent used manure spreader for months, but why did he have to call now?

"It's a good one, is it?"

"Ya, real good. Completely restored and hardly ever been used. It's amazing for its age."

"How old is it?"

"Well, it's about forty years old, but you'd never guess it standing here looking at it."

"ARE YOU CRAZY?" I yelled, no longer able to control myself. "YOU WANT FIFTEEN HUNDRED BUCKS FOR A FORTY-YEAR-OLD MANURE SPREADER. YOU'VE GOTTA BE KIDDING."

There must have been something in how I said it because whoever it was on the other end said something unrepeatable and hung up. I was furious. I could feel myself all itchy and sweaty and red in the face as I handed the receiver back to Swami Radha.

"The nerve of some people," I exclaimed. "You wouldn't believe what that guy just tried to do," and I quickly told her what had happened. "These guys have to realize. Just because I live in an ashram doesn't mean I can be taken for a ride. I've been buying and selling machinery for years. You'd be surprised what goes on, I can tell you."

Once again, my voice gave me away. I could hear it all: self-justification, defending, even the strident tone of righteous indignation. No one would ever take me for a ride, that's for sure!

Swami Radha was sitting in her favorite high-backed chair, gently rocking, listening, nodding occasionally, not saying a word. Suddenly she stopped and leaned forward.

"DON'T YOU GO SPREADING YOUR MANURE AROUND HERE!"

She looked at me intently, her eyes flashing, then sat back in her chair and gently resumed rocking. A tiny hint of a smile appeared at the corners of her mouth. I started to breathe again.

A few weeks later we were walking along the road to the storage building at the far end of the ashram when she raised what sounded like a fairly general question.

"Can you listen to women?" she asked.

It was a gray, overcast day in late spring. The temperature had dropped during the night, foreshadowing a storm, and I could feel the damp, chilly air cutting through my thin sweater.

"Very well," I replied. "In fact I can listen to women much easier than I can to men."

Silence filled the space between us. I thought she probably just wanted to test me out, see if I could really listen to women. I was glad to be able to reassure her that indeed I could. As we entered the storage building my attention turned to other things and I gave no more thought to her question.

A few days later I was at Many Mansions wrestling an extremely heavy chest of drawers into a corner of the sunroom when she suddenly turned to me and said, "Can you listen to women?"

Her voice seemed a little sharp this time which puzzled me. Perhaps she had forgotten having asked me the same question not so long ago. I hastened to reassure her once again, this time with the intention of removing all doubt. However, my desire to reassure her only made matters worse. So intent was the desire that I failed to hear what I was actually saying.

"I listen to women very well," I said. "In fact I prefer the company of a woman any day. I love talking to women."

I had always thought my hearing was good. I had grown up in an atmosphere that had trained my hearing to be acutely sensitive to the merest suggestion of criticism, imagined or otherwise. I could hear criticism as clearly as a sleeping dog can hear a stranger's footstep, and I tended to react in the same way. Hearing was key to my survival and it puzzled me that Swami Radha seemed to doubt my ability to hear. I had never questioned it.

The third time she asked left little doubt that I simply wasn't listening. I couldn't hear what was behind her question because I didn't want to hear. The only way she could get past my intentional deafness was to keep asking until the light dawned. How else could she as a woman tell a man that there was an area where he needed to do some serious reflection, without risking the wrath of his injured male pride?

My mind went back to our road trip and the night she told me about Wolfgang getting caught by the Gestapo. I remember being shocked when she asked if men thought that women didn't have anything intelligent to say. Maybe some men thought that but I was hardly ready to include myself among them. Now I wondered. Why had it been necessary for her to ask me the same question three times? Why, if I was as good a listener as I claimed to be? For sure, it had something to do with my attitude towards women, but because of a self-deception that was rapidly becoming more apparent, I had no idea what my attitude was or how I truly felt about women.

Only occasionally would I allow myself to listen to my heart, and even then it was hard to trust what I heard. Yet the message was always the same.

"You've got to let it go. You've got to soften up and let it go."

As with the unfortunate salesman trying to sell the manure spreader over the phone—what was I defending? What does it matter? He's just another guy trying to survive. Why do I think I'm any different?

Arrogance by definition sees no need to reflect upon itself. Thus I failed to hear or take seriously what was at the heart of Swami Radha's question to me about listening to women. For her it was not just a question. It had been an attempt to stimulate me into investigating a cherished belief about myself in order to determine what was true, rather than continue with a self-deception that in all likelihood was the root of considerable pain and sorrow. She had already told me a number of times, and in many different ways, that intellectual pride was a very serious obstacle to spiritual growth.

Swami Radha thought that if I could hear myself I might come to realize how much my habits of speech were preventing me from hearing anything but the demands of my ego. Not long after the phone call in the sunroom she told me about a practice of mauna (silence) that could be a very fruitful experiment if I wanted to try it. I heard her, all right, but the thought of self-imposed silence made me agitated and anxious. I was shocked by my physical reaction to the idea. Whenever I imagined what it would be like not to be able to speak, I would start to itch and my hands would turn clammy as if the choice to do an intentional spiritual practice was somehow tantamount to putting myself into a glass prison. Obviously the way I used speech was closely connected to some idea I had about freedom and not getting caught again.

Swami Radha waited and observed. After some time, when she saw how disturbing silence was for me, she suggested that I watch how I used my time, instead.

"Keep a little notebook with you throughout your day," she said, "and every fifteen minutes stop what you're doing and jot down a few key words noting how you're using your time. And do the experiment for thirty days."

That's all. Nothing about speech or anxiety-producing psychological impediments—just try an experiment and see where it takes you. It led me to a sobering realization: I was losing countless hours of precious time generating speech that for the most part was serving the emotional needs of a big ego. At least she was spared the difficulty of having to say it to me directly.

Still, I continued to have difficulty hearing her. Whenever her piercing discrimination threatened to undo my illusions my hearing would almost literally cease to function, a response that helped to preserve my illusions far longer than necessary. I even think Swami Radha was considering the possibility that there might also be a physiological basis to my poor hearing; that is, until we made the recording together.

On a warm, sultry August afternoon Swami Radha came down to the studio at Many Mansions to read and record some poems she had written over many years of spiritual aspiration. Some of the poems describe her most intimate moments with Divine Mother or Krishna; others spare nothing of the harsher realities of spiritual life. As with all of her writing, the poems reflect her deep personal experience. I felt very privileged when she asked me to record her reading them on that warm, summer afternoon. It is one of my most precious memories of working intimately with her.

The recording studio on the first floor of Many Mansions at the back of the house looks out over the lake. It may have the best view of any recording studio in the world, but it can get a little warm in the afternoon with the sun pouring through the windows. I found that if I left the windows and sliding glass door open on days like this, it was still possible to record without any serious noise distractions from outside. The midday heat usually suppressed sounds that would otherwise have been picked up by the microphones.

Swami Radha was in the middle of reading one of the early poems when I first heard the sound of the boat over the studio monitor. As soon as she finished reading, I called through the studio monitor to ask her to wait until the boat passed. She looked at the two women who were sitting across from her. Then she looked at me behind the glass window of the control room.

"What boat?" she asked.

No one in the room had heard it. The two women looked at each other and shrugged as if to say, Well, you know he doesn't seem to hear very well at the best of times. I started to squirm, thinking, Oh no, it's my wandering mind again, this time hearing things that aren't even there, when suddenly the sound of the boat entered the room again. This time everyone heard it. Through the glass Swami Radha gave me one of her intent looks, but didn't say anything for a moment. Then she started to chuckle.

"So, you hear very well after all. Isn't that interesting." Pause. "Well, I am glad you're looking after the recording."

With that we started to come together again. For once her work had been more important to me than the almighty integrity of my stone-deaf ego. A little event on a warm summer afternoon, with major implications for the future.

I'm sure intellectual pride was at the root of my resistance to her.

Intellectual pride with its shield of arrogance stops the flow of love cold and turns the feminine away from the door. Radha as Cosmic Love, one of the most alluring feminine forms to grace sacred mythology, holds the key to life's biggest mystery: Why was I born? What is the purpose of my life? Swami Radha held the key and she knew the way, and she invited me to come close and find out for myself. Even today I wonder at how I resisted her invitation for so long.

Swami Radha recognized that confusion can be part of the ego's defense system. She would keep the light going, observe its effect, watch carefully, and taking her cues from my responses, we would either take another step closer to the truth, or she would pull back and change the focus completely, and wait for another opportunity to arise. In some cases, as with the gift of the ballpoint pen, that meant having to wait years until I was receptive enough to hear her. One time I apologized for being so tortoise-like as I reflected on the state of my mind during one of those dense phases.

"Never mind," she said. "At least the tortoise will get there. Shooting stars? We've had lots of those. Here today, gone tomorrow, and what good have they done? No. I would rather have the tortoise anytime."

King David

H alloo," cried the voice behind me as I walked along the road in front of Many Mansions. I turned and saw Swami Radha standing near the entrance to her house fifty feet away.

"What do you know about King David?" she called out to me.

"King who?" I asked, turning towards her.

"David!" she said. "King David danced before the Lord. Did you know that?"

"King David," I muttered as I walked up the sidewalk towards Many Mansions. "How would I know anything about King David?"

"King David danced before the Lord," she said again as I drew near. "There's a lot of power in a name. You should find out what your name means. It was given to you. Could it have been a message?"

I had never thought of my name as a message but now I wanted to find out. That night I read about King David in the Old Testament and discovered a hidden wealth behind the name. His story is a marvelous allegory of the dangers and pitfalls facing any aspirant on the spiritual path who has a powerful ego.

David, the young shepherd, was called upon by God to destroy the enemies of His chosen people and restore His covenant with them. David, successor to Saul, the jealous king whose all-consuming hatred of his young successor finally ended in a paroxysm of self-destruction. David, the Chosen One whose obedience to the will of God was sorely tested throughout his life.

David's ascendancy to the throne of Israel was virtually assured after he killed the giant Philistine by catapulting a rock into the giant's forehead right between the eyes. The victory heralded certain defeat for the Philistines and demonstrated to the Israelites that the young shepherd also had the courage to be their king. Whether or not he could sustain the moral requirements of that high office once caught in the throes of temptation was another question. After his affair with Bathsheba, the beautiful wife of one of his soldiers, David ordered her husband sent into a battle under circumstances that made his death almost certain. Once Bathsheba's husband was out of the picture, David took her as his wife. As a result of these actions his life became an endless round of battle against the forces of retribution that rose up against him. When he died at the age of seventy after forty years on the throne of Israel, David was satisfied that he had kept God's commandment to protect the Israelites, though he had not been able to fulfill God's request to build the temple. In the end David "...returned to the earth from which he had come" leaving his only son, Solomon, to pick up the pieces and repair the kingdom. Solomon completed the temple, thus restoring God to His primary place in the Cosmos. It is a wonderful irony of the divine play that Solomon was the son born of David's adulterous union with Bathsheba. So what does all this say to me about the evolution of Consciousness and dancing before the Lord?

In the late eighties when Swami Radha asked me to oversee the construction of the Temple of Light in the ashram, I thought about David immediately. Why? Where had he gone wrong? And what did it mean that Solomon, the illegitimate son, would end up being the one to build the temple? As literal history the story is questionable but as reflection it could be immediately relevant. As with the crowned gods and goddesses of the Kundalini system*, the Old Testament idea of king could also represent the same thing—Higher Consciousness. Com-

* See: Swami Sivananda Radha, *Kundalini Yoga for the West.*

mon sense tells us that there is a lot of power in awareness; one who is aware and conscious can have considerable influence over others. But it is also true that abuse of that power has serious repercussions, particularly in the spiritual field where a neophyte's trust and naïveté make her or him extremely vulnerable. For me, the question coming out of David's story was the same one Swami Radha posed to anyone coming to her for the teachings: Can you learn from the mistakes of others?

Soon after Swami Radha introduced me to the Old Testament king a situation arose in the ashram that raised this challenge. Two long-time disciples of Swami Radha, both mantra initiates, gravitated together in a romantic liaison. The subsequent developments around this incident showed me how far Swami Radha would go to try to save wavering disciples from falling into the abyss.

"It is not enough for a man to have the title of king," she said to me during one of our discussions about the situation. "He must also act like a king. The people are not stupid. They watch what their king does and they will not for long allow themselves to be led by one who is unwilling to live up to even their basic standards of acceptable behavior."

We were talking about a man who for several years had been a powerful leader in the ashram. Now he was on his way out, asked to leave the ashram because he had repeatedly gone against the principles he espoused in the classroom by using his position and his considerable charm to exploit women sexually. Finally, after trying everything imaginable to save his spiritual life, Swami Radha brought the whole thing to an end. I watched it happen, indeed was part of the process, and could see that it saddened her terribly. In the final days, as the situation reached its peak, she became very fierce and Kali-like*, as he floundered in the confusion brought on by his instincts.

First she called the woman into the sunroom at Many Mansions. Their talk was brief and to the point. Swami Radha made it clear that

---

*Kali, a goddess who symbolically devours her creation in order to create anew.

the woman had to find out what she really wanted in her life. If it was a man she wanted then the ashram and spiritual life were not the place to find one. The woman was given three months to figure it out in another yoga center far away from the ashram and any contact with Swami Radha. She left the next day, badly shaken and confused but with an objective and a time frame that allowed her hope but left little room for ambiguity.

Swami Radha then turned her attention to the man, a disciple of hers for many years.

"You are to go into seclusion for thirty days," she said. "Use the small cabin by the creek and I will see that food is left at the door each day. You are to have no contact with anyone and you are to use the time exclusively for reflection and spiritual practice. This time you must decide about the future of your spiritual life. Om Namah Sivaya*."

And that was it for both of them. In short, their spiritual lives were on the line and Swami Radha had been forced to take extreme action.

Swami Radha always said that it is the generosity of Divine Mother to give us this lifetime to undo the mistakes of the past, and she tried to practice this principle with her students. But in this situation the time for allowances was over. For the man in particular, too many allowances had already been made.

Barely a week had gone by, however, before the lunch and supper trays left by the cabin door began to include samples of home baking prepared exclusively for him by the kitchen coordinator, who apparently had been harboring a secret longing for several years. When the cookies appeared the secret was out. Swami Radha read the signs and within forty-eight hours it was over: the man was gone, the cook was gone, and those of us who did not understand what was happening were left deeply shaken by their sudden departures. On the morning

---

*"Siva" is the destroyer aspect of God. The mantra *Om Namah Sivaya* calls on Siva to destroy the obstacles that stand in the way of spiritual growth.

he was supposed to leave the ashram, Swami Radha called me into the sunroom to tell me.

"You take him to the ferry landing," she said, her face ashen and worn, "and give him this note."

That was all. I said I would and left to make arrangements. My mind whirled with the implications of being the messenger. Men stick together, men support each other, this seems so extreme, why has it come to this, could the same thing happen to me? I kept saying, "I have got to trust the Light and try to understand what is happening," but the words felt empty and meaningless.

Sadness and confusion continued to spin around inside me as I drove the man to the ferry landing five kilometers away.

"Where are you going?" I asked.

"Toronto for now."

"What will you do?"

"I've arranged to stay with friends. After that I don't know."

"Swami Radha asked me to give you this."

I handed him the note. He glanced at it, folded it, put it into his shirt pocket, and stared ahead without saying a word. There was nothing more I could say or do except wish him luck. I stayed in the car while he walked down the ramp towards the boat, his heavy suitcase bumping against his right leg as if trying to hurry him along. Finally he was swallowed up by the traffic driving onto the boat and that was the last I saw of him. When the ferry started to pull away from the dock, I turned around and drove back up the road towards the ashram. Behind me the sunlight filtered through the trees along the roadside and the air coming through the open window was cool and refreshing. I remembered that I had planned to service the tractor before lunch. I looked at my watch. Still time to do it, I thought, as I turned off the highway onto the road leading to the ashram.

That afternoon Swami Radha called the residents to Many Mansions. She wanted to bring everyone up to date on what had happened and why, and to make very clear what the limits were. There were about twenty people gathered in the room when Swami Radha came in. We chanted a mantra for a few minutes to clear the air, then she began to speak. Nothing she said that afternoon fit any of my cherished notions about love, but then nothing from the previous two weeks had either. It was the beginning of my own departure out of sentimentality towards the kind of thinking that reflects sharp discrimination and an honest, gut-level appraisal of the facts.

"Everyone comes here by divine appointment and for this reason they are given a long rein in which to find their way. However, if a person makes a commitment past the two-year residency period, then I start to make demands on him, or on her, because it is my spiritual duty to strengthen aspirants. The Divine will not support anything that goes against that commitment.

"Please think about this. A man who needs women, who puts a woman in a certain position in order to satisfy his own needs, will later resent her for having given him the power to use her. For the sake of the woman *and* the man, I cannot support any behavior that undermines and tries to betray the promises they have individually made to the Most High. I cannot and will not. And the same goes for the rest of you. Therefore, I am asking that the men and women residents of the ashram begin a tapas* that will limit your talk with each other strictly to business matters. In other words, except about work-related matters in the ashram there will be no talking between the men and women who live here. I have to say that to make such a rule goes against everything I stand for with respect to the teachings and our particular way of living them here. I did not, under any circumstances, want it to come to this. But if I don't do it, Krishna will. And believe me, He would be a lot harder on you than I ever could be—a lot harder, because of the promises you have made."

After the meeting, I felt stunned and confused. As I walked up the

---

*An observance or an abstention practiced to increase awareness.

road from Many Mansions, my mind spun like a dervish trying to make sense of what I thought was a drastic response to a very human situation. I could accept that my confusion reflected ignorance of the whole picture, but it also indicated that some pretty fundamental issues had been stirred up in me as well. I kept walking, trying to think it through, trying to walk perspective and balance back into my mind, trying to surrender and accept that Swami Radha knew what she was doing, that somehow the Light had brought all this to the fore. Maybe, but how? And how could I trust this so-called neutral energy to do the right thing?

After awhile the situation began to clear. I could see that Swami Radha had taken strong action to protect a fundamental principle of her teachings. Indeed, the integrity of the teachings came first for her, far above being liked and accepted by anyone. That was one of the qualities that had made her so trustworthy for me in the beginning. Now, the more I thought about her integrity, the more my illusions about love and relationship began to wash away. Thankfully, one of the first to start being dislodged was the myth of male omnipotence.

When it came to guiding her devotees, Swami Radha could be very pragmatic. She recognized and was very accepting of our propensity to make mistakes, to fall victim to our basic natures, and encouraged us to keep going in spite of the mistakes.

"You can learn from the mistakes of others, or you can learn from trial and error," she often said. "The choice is yours. But if the same error keeps occurring over and over, then it is a different matter."

Indeed it was. In that case her patient tolerance would ignite into strong action, whatever it took to preserve a devotee's Light no matter how faint it had become. Swami Radha said many times that true awareness means being willing to "see yourself at the gut level"—looking at what is, not just at what you want to see. But she also acknowledged that few aspirants have the courage or willingness to question their own illusions with such intense honesty.

"The ones who can't do it," she said, "have their illusions challenged by life itself, and it's a much more painful way to learn. For some there is no other way and for this reason the path can look very cruel indeed."

That evening after our meeting at Many Mansions I went to visit Swami Radha in the sunroom. I found her alone sitting in front of her TV completely absorbed in a CNN news story, her orange juice, vitamin C, and a few biscuits with cheese on a small plastic tray in front of her. She motioned for me to sit in the chair beside her as she helped herself to a biscuit. Supper. I had interrupted her supper. A little nervous, I sat down and began to watch the news as well.

Soon her powers of concentration intensified the atmosphere between us. It was often like this coming into her company. She was always interested in the practical, day-to-day matters of living in the ashram, but only a small part of her mind would get involved in the details. The rest of her mind would be listening, watching, waiting to see what the Divine Committee had in store, or what the Flute Player's* song was going to be. What would be considered a casual visit in any other setting was for her an opportunity to serve. That is what seemed to be foremost on her mind as she clicked off the TV, swiveled in her chair and looked directly at me.

"You're here. That's good. It's easier to see what needs doing when you're close by. I've been thinking about this because with the farm work you're always at the far end of the ashram. You can come closer, you know."

Swami Radha smiled and looked at me closely.

"So. What's on your mind?"

"Well, I've been thinking about the meeting and what you said about men and women, and it's left me feeling confused. I understand what you're doing here, but still I don't know if everyone does."

"That could be. But you see, David, I am not one for making rules.

---

*Krishna

That is the last thing I want to do because it really goes against the grain in me. That is why there is so much freedom in the ashram. There has to be that freedom for people to find their own way. But I have also seen over the years that very few people have the discipline it takes to handle that kind of freedom. They just don't. And for this reason you end up with what they have in the monasteries and some of the other religious communities I have visited. There the monks and the nuns have rules for everything—set times for working, for sleeping, for eating, for meditating, for prayer—you name it. Why? Because the people who live in these settings need the structure that rules provide. But then the responsibility is outside of themselves, you see."

Swami Radha paused to eat one of the biscuits on the tray in front of her.

"Celibacy was never meant to be a lifelong vow," she said, "although that is what it becomes for some people. Rather, it is a spiritual practice that is undertaken in order to conserve energy that is undergoing a process of transformation. It's not that sex is sin—I have never said that. For me, sin is the intentional repetition of mistakes once they are known. No, celibacy is practiced so that energy normally used to satisfy the instincts can be directed to a higher purpose."

Just before I left, Swami Radha reached up and gave me a hug.

"You have to strengthen your mind and your discrimination in order to stand on your own feet," she said. "Otherwise what will happen after I die?"

One morning, a few weeks after our visit, Swami Radha called to ask if I could drive her to Nelson for a meeting. I said yes, of course, thrilled to have the time alone with her away from the ashram and happy just to be able to help in some way.

"We'll have lunch," she said. "You may remember Elsa Warner. Well, she is in Nelson and wants to meet with me, so this is a good opportunity for you to see how things work. We'll need to catch the next ferry, though."

The trip to Nelson, a small city situated on the west arm of Kootenay Lake, takes about an hour from the time you leave the ashram. You first have to cross the lake by ferry, then drive the twenty miles or so along the curving shoreline highway into town. It's always a pleasant trip even in bad weather, and it doesn't seem to make any difference whether you're in a hurry to keep an appointment in town or returning home again at a more leisurely pace—the travel time never varies more than a minute or two either way. I'm not sure why that is except to say that the road and the ferry seem to have a kind of cooperative sensibility between them. Only once have I seen the ferry unable to dock and that was because of dangerous high winds. Not taking any chances, the little boat, filled end to end with cars and passengers, retreated to a lee at the harbor entrance and waited out the passing storm.

As we drove along the highway into Nelson, Swami Radha read articles aloud from a newsmagazine. It was like her to use the opportunity to check in with the world, but I knew the magazine was also a foil. She used newsmagazines to occupy her busy mind while another part of her mind focused on the divine play at hand. It was a sunny fall day, warm with just a slight breeze. Yellow leaves scurried across the road in front of us and the sun sparkled through the branches overhead. We were in no hurry; the appointment was still an hour away.

Swami Radha was relaxed and thoughtful as we crossed the orange bridge heading into the city. So far she had said nothing about the lunch meeting other than the fact that Elsa had written to her about "...wanting to make up for past mistakes." I had the impression that Swami Radha was not about to rush into forgiveness quickly. Experience had made her very aware of the oscillations of fanciful minds. In the silence between us, it occurred to me that I could learn a great deal in the next few hours simply by watching and keeping quiet.

Rose's, a European delicatessen and gift emporium where she could always find "just the right thing," was Swami Radha's favorite restaurant in town. Elsa Warner was seated at the counter waiting for us. She turned to look when a mixed chorus of smiles and respectful greetings from the owner and his wife announced the arrival of their special customer once again. This, I thought to myself, is an impeccably ordered event. Only the Flute Player* could have arranged the details so perfectly.

The conversation at lunch seemed low-key and somewhat general. Swami Radha asked Elsa about her life, how her work was going, questions that reflected interest and concern but not so personal that they would create undue pressure. It soon became clear to me that Swami Radha had no vested interest in the outcome of this meeting, which of course allowed her to see a much broader picture than the conversation suggested. I noticed that Elsa was guarded and cautious, responding with just enough information to satisfy the inquiry but not a lot more.

A few more tries, then Swami Radha suddenly switched the subject to a musician friend of hers who lived in the United States, an accomplished pianist who had recently talked to her about the possibility of doing a tour in Canada. In fact, he was already planning the tour and had some tentative bookings. What Swami Radha wanted to know from Elsa was if she could do anything to arrange a performance in Winnipeg, the city where she lived. Elsa had a few ideas, but since she was only peripherally connected to the arts and entertainment scene in the city she felt she didn't have much to offer. Swami Radha prodded a bit more, encouraging whatever embers of intuitive understanding might still be glowing in the woman's heart.

As I watched and listened I began to see what Swami Radha was doing and I marveled at the simplicity and consideration in her approach. There was nothing threatening in what she said—no ultimatums, no conditions, no recriminations—just a simple request to help

* Krishna.

a friend achieve an artistic goal. Ultimately the decision to help or not to help was entirely in Elsa's hands, but how she responded would give Swami Radha an accurate measure of how serious she was about making amends.

In time it became evident that she wasn't that serious. Elsa returned to Winnipeg and was never heard from again. I don't know what she thought, but whatever expectations she may have had concerning her relationship with Swami Radha appeared to fade quickly once they were put to the test. Without knowing it, Elsa had been spared any karmic repercussions because of Swami Radha's willingness to allow the process to unfold in whatever way it was meant to.

Swami Radha, too, lost nothing in the process. In fact we all gained something. It was an excellent lunch and the two of us had a wonderful visit on our way home that afternoon.

"Never use the force of your personality or your position to try and convince anyone," she said, as we drove onto the ferry that would take us back to Kootenay Bay. "If you do, you become an authority and if people base their decisions on that authority, their resentment will come back at you many times over. Try to remember that. It's not a lesson you want to learn the hard way."

CHAPTER FIFTEEN

Krishna's Flute

Krishna's Lila—the dance of creation between the manifest and the unmanifest, the seen and the unseen, sometimes called the Rasa Lila—continued to play itself out for the rest of that summer and into fall. In early September, after taking Alicia back to school in Victoria, Donna and I stopped at Bartels, an Indian food wholesaler on Main Street in Vancouver, to pick up a bulk order for the ashram kitchen. While Donna worked out the details of the order with a clerk from the store, I wandered off by myself to look around. Just the smells alone made the stop worthwhile. Barrels of cardamom, curry, dal, cans of chutney, fruit, mangoes, elephant gods piled in a corner, blue gods on the wall, mighty goddesses on the backs of lions, brass pots, brass lamps, trays of sweets, cotton sacks of lentils and rice piled high on the floor—this store, for me, breathed the essence of India from every square inch of floor space, including the Canada Post office at the rear of the store that doubled as a video outlet for Indian films.

I stared at the rows of brightly colored video covers behind the counter and thought about Swami Radha. In recent weeks she had been going through a hard time with recurrent arthritis and I thought that since she loved Indian dancing maybe I could find something here she would like—a dance film, perhaps, that would help take her mind off the pain. The problem was all the video covers looked the same. How could I tell what was inside?

I was staring hard at the covers trying to find a way around this problem when a young East Indian man came out of the back room and asked if there was anything he could do to help.

"Well, maybe. I'm looking for a film about Indian dance, if you have anything like that. I have a friend who loves Indian dancing."

The young man turned to the shelves behind him.

"I don't know," he said, "they're all pretty good. Lots of them have dancing and music, you know. It's kind of popular with many people. So...."

Then he reached down and took a video off one of the lower shelves. It was called *Gopal Krishna*. On its cover, as with all the other videos in the store, was the same full-face close-up of the handsome male actor with the adoring female in the background. However, in one respect this one was different. Instead of wielding a sword or swinging a club, the actor wore a crown and held a flute to his lips.

"This one is supposed to be pretty good," said the young man. "I mean, I don't know that myself but my father said it was good. He told me it has lots of singing and dancing and he likes that, you know, like the bhajans and kirtans and the satsanga. He's always having the satsanga at home and his friends...uh...they like to come over for it. I think they just like to have an excuse to visit." The young man looked down and smiled to himself. "Mind you, I don't care much for all this devotional stuff myself. It's more for the old people, you know."

I nodded and told him I would buy the video if it was for sale.

That night back in the ashram I stopped by Many Mansions and gave it to Swami Radha.

"I don't know if it's any good," I said apologetically. "I really hope you understand, I'm not at all sure...so don't feel you have to watch it or anything."

Finally I shut up and left Swami Radha to figure out for herself whether she liked the film or not.

The next morning one of her close disciples came out to the garden where I was working.

"Swami Radha wants to see you," he said. "She stayed up late watching the film you brought for her. Then this morning she told me that she'd watched it again during the night when she wasn't able to sleep. She loves it. Already she seems better."

Of course I was delighted to hear that. I dropped what I was doing and hurried over to Many Mansions to see her. She appeared tired and I could see how painful the arthritis was by the way she walked over to her chair. A small portable TV sat on a rolling table close to her bed, the empty *Gopal Krishna* video box beside it.

"This is very good," she said. "I have watched it now a couple of times and I'm going to see it again. I will probably have a sleep first. But I wonder, how did you know what it was?"

"I didn't, Swami Radha. I asked for a film about Indian dancing because I knew how much you liked the dancing. The man said there was lots of music and dancing on this one, and that's about it. It was just good luck, I guess."

"Perhaps. But it tells me something else, too. Have you ever thought what it would mean to be Krishna's friend? Can you think what that might mean?"

I didn't know how to answer that and Swami Radha wasn't expecting me to answer it then and there. But the question stirred me because being a friend of Krishna would mean being Radha's friend too. There wouldn't be any separation among us. So that was a start. But as with the film there was more to the story than that.

As cinematography the *Gopal Krishna* film can easily be found wanting. The screenplay relies heavily on melodramatic dialogue to convey complex interconnected themes and the emotional range of the leading actors is limited. Also, since the film had not originally been produced for export, the Hindi dialect remains and there are no subtitles.

But all that is beside the point. The film was one of hundreds on the shelf and there had been no way to assess its merit other than through the testimony of a person who hadn't seen it. Yet the video turned out to be an accurate and delightful rendering of the legends of Krishna. Also, as the young man's father had said, the music and dance scenes were splendid.

Only a few minutes into the film, Swami Radha easily recognized the stories from her readings about the life of Krishna. But more important, she realized that the video was a confirmation, in the same way that some of her dreams in the past had been confirmations, that she was doing the right thing, that she was not alone in her work. Krishna may not write huge letters in the sky but that didn't mean he wouldn't use a video. Over and over she had seen that Krishna would use whatever was available to get the message to his beloved Radha.

Gopala was the name given to Krishna in his early childhood and adolescence growing up in the idyllic pastoral village of Brindavan. Gopala is the adopted son of the cowherd Nanda. According to legend, he is the youthful Krishna, mischievous stealer of gopi's hearts, the imp who loved butter so much that he and his friends were constantly stealing it from the gopis. Invariably in the scramble at the scene of the crime a few butter pots would get broken—Krishna repeatedly smashing our tightly held convictions and cherished beliefs. Above all he is a trusted friend, loved by everyone in the village, especially by Radha.

Krishna's Brindavan period is a potent metaphor for spiritual growth. Even before birth, Krishna is tested by Kamsa, the evil uncle who imprisons Krishna's father and mother and threatens to destroy any children they might have in order to claim the kingdom that is rightfully Krishna's. Kamsa is symbolic for the ego—pretender to the throne of Higher Consciousness. As such, he manifests a multitude of personalities whose task is to undermine and eventually destroy the Higher Self that is Krishna in us. With each victory Krishna grows stronger until the day comes when he must confront the ego itself and destroy it. Only when he has done that can Krishna leave his childhood behind to assume the crown that is rightfully his.

As allegory, the legends of Gopal Krishna are unsurpassed. On the right line of spiritual life, with a proper foundation in discrimination, our awareness will eventually grow into an invincible force for preserving the Light of Consciousness. Along the way, as the legends assert, we are tested over and over.

When I finally saw the film I was struck by one scene in particular in relation to what I understood was a severe testing time for Swami Radha. This is the scene when Krishna leaves Brindavan to go to Mathura to fight the evil king, Kamsa. On the road leading out of the village Krishna is forced to stop his chariot because of a body lying across the road. He jumps down from the chariot and runs to help only to discover to his horror that it is Radha, his beloved. Distraught that Krishna is leaving after their years of growing up together in Brindavan, Radha has thrown herself down on the road, hoping this will be enough to get Krishna to change his mind and return to the village. But of course he can't. Krishna is compelled to do his duty. He must fight Kamsa to the death as he has promised to do.

The scene is emotionally charged. It is, after all, their physical separation, which for lovers is unbearable. But the scene speaks of separation on another level as well. Radha's separation from Krishna represents the separation of individual consciousness from Cosmic Consciousness, which for many of us is experienced as an unbearable longing that comes from having heard the flute, the sound of God, and not being able to respond. It is as hard for Krishna as it is for Radha. The scene ends with Krishna giving Radha his flute. Then he gets back into his chariot and drives on, leaving Radha standing by the side of the road holding the flute in her hand. The message is clear: Radha has been given the power to be Krishna's instrument on earth. In the language of metaphor, she has realized the power of the mantra.

"You be the flute," Swami Radha often said to me, "and let Krishna play the melody."

Over time, Swami Radha gradually recovered from this particular bout of arthritis and resumed her busy schedule in the ashram. Although it was good to see her active again, the recent illness had forced me to accept the fact that she wouldn't be with us forever. Acceptance was a beginning, but the need to do more was brought home to me one day at lunch when she told a group of us at her table a story she had been reading that morning. It was the story of Krishna's despair over Radha's death. As she told it I listened intensely, trying to retain every word as though I had only this one chance to hear. Afterwards, I wrote the story down as I remembered it.

The day came when Yama, the Lord of Death and King of Hell, called out to Radha.

"Why don't you give up this Krishna?" he said. "Don't you see he is teasing you? He's not serious. He doesn't mean it. Why don't you give up this Krishna now?"

Radha said, "No. I have to see Krishna once more."

"What is this crazy love?" Yama asked, for he had never seen anything like it before.

But all Radha could say was, "I just have to see Krishna again." This made Yama even more curious.

"Radha," he said, "I want to know what that love is. I shall give you three days to see Krishna but then you must come back here."

Radha got up to take her leave.

As she turned the Lord of Death asked, "How are you going to come back? What manner of death will you choose? Fire? Steel? Poison? Water?"

Radha said, "I have heard that water is most gentle."

Radha returned to Mathura to see Krishna one last time. The Lord was extremely happy to see her.

He said, "Let's go to the Island of Enchantment. There will be only you and I there, together forever."

But Radha said, "No. We can't do that. You have promised your friends and these promises you must keep. I have promised to fulfill a job and I, too, must keep my promise."

Krishna did not know what Radha's destiny was.

He said, "All right. When all the tournaments are over we shall discuss it."

But he did not know this discussion would never take place.

Now it happened that Radha had to return to Yama on the same day that Krishna was to be crowned King of Mathura. Although Krishna was born a Brahman, his father, Vasudeva, told the people that the ceremony recognizing his son as a Brahman had never been performed.

Accordingly, the decision was made to have the ceremony and a charioteer was dispatched to the Ganges to get some holy water. Along the way the charioteer spotted Radha walking along the roadside and stopped to ask if he could be of any assistance.

Radha, very tired, turned to the charioteer and said, "Would you give me a lift to the river?"

"Of course," said the charioteer. "I am going there myself. I am on an errand for Krishna."

And Radha said, "Yes. I am, too."

When they reached the bank of the river, Radha got down from the chariot and waited for the charioteer to depart. Then without any further hesitation, she walked into the river and was drowned. At precisely that moment, far away in Mathura, a hermit standing near Krishna turned to him and said, "You will never see Radha again."

Krishna was shocked. "Why do you say that? It cannot be. Where is she? Where is Radha?"

He began to search the crowd frantically. When she was nowhere to be seen, Krishna ran to his own chariot and raced off to the Ganges. But of course by the time he got to the banks of the sacred river, Radha was gone. A yogi standing on the bank watched Krishna walk into the river crying out Radha's name over and over as he desperately searched for her body.

"What do you want with her body?" he asked the Lord. "She is gone. Your friend, the great white bird, Garuda, came and lifted her onto his back and carried her away to Goloka."

Krishna looked at the yogi and then far out over the water.

"Radha!" he cried. "Can you not show your face to me once more?"

In the distance, above the mountains on the opposite shore, Krishna saw a white bird—the spirit of Radha—soaring high above the peaks.

"Can you not come back?" he cried. "Can you not be my queen?"

The spirit of Radha called back to him, "No, Krishna. Our time on earth is finished. You will have your queen in Mathura. And one day you will meet another dark-haired girl who will be your Radha once again."

Swami Radha slowly looked around the table at each one of us. She was quiet, serious, letting the story settle. Her eyes were like deep black pools. After a couple of minutes she began to explain how the story of Radha could be understood as an allegory for the birth and death cycle of creation. I listened, but at the same time was filled with a deep, penetrating sadness. I knew she was using the story to help prepare us for her own death.

"The story of Radha's death tells us that the whole cycle of creation will start again," she said, "but that something else endures throughout all the beginnings and endings over many lifetimes. In part, this is the message that is meant to be conveyed through the love play of Radha and Krishna. The water of life evaporates from the ocean of creation, rising up to its source. The raindrops that eventually return to the earth fill the sacred rivers flowing into the sea. Symbolically, Radha is the drop in the deep. She will always return to the deep, there to begin the whole cycle again.

"Somehow it is our separation from this basic principle of life and death, birth and creation, beginning and end, that compels us to keep trying to fulfill the cycle through union with a beloved. Like Krishna in the story, so enamored are we with creation, that we have momentarily forgotten who we are. It is Radha's duty to remind us again and again.

"So that is why I keep on with all of you," she laughed. "Because you *can* make it in one lifetime, you can. I just have to keep reminding you. Om Om."

CHAPTER SIXTEEN

Divine Mother

One night when I was over at Many Mansions, Swami Radha talked at some length about her mother. For as long I had known her, she had never spoken much about her mother beyond describing the physical beauty that masked her mother's deep-seated jealousy and fear. So fearful was she of being abandoned by her husband once she was no longer physically attractive to him, that she tried unsuccessfully to abort her only child in the early stages of pregnancy.

"I didn't find out that my mother had tried to abort me until my teens when I was learning all the things girls were taught at that time: sewing, embroidery, knitting, and what have you. I learned these skills quickly and well—everything except knitting. I could not do it. Every time I picked up the knitting needles to try I would start to cry and I just didn't know what was wrong. Then one time when I was home from school, it came out in a conversation with one of the servants who had looked after me as a baby that my mother had tried to abort me using a knitting needle. When I heard this I understood at last what was wrong.

"Now, I could take this fundamental fact and, year after year for the rest of my life, turn it into a tragic story in order to elicit sympathy. Or I could look back in a very different way at my mother and ask, What could have made her want to do this?

"Of course there were lots of possible reasons. Her fear of being left by my father might have compelled her to this extreme action. He did, after all, have his mistresses. But for whatever reason, changing the way I thought about this myself made it possible for me to forgive her. Eventually I was able to show others how to approach forgiveness by trying very hard to understand the other. From this and from many other experiences in my life, I have learned how to use the experiences of the past as a basis for my teaching."

Swami Radha paused to stir a tiny spoonful of vitamin C powder into a glass of orange juice. The vitamin was part of a daily regimen she had begun years ago to combat her severe arthritis. She sipped the juice, then continued with her story.

"As far as my relationship to my mother was concerned, it was never close. After the war I wrote to her asking if we could meet again, but she wrote back saying, no, she did not want to see me. After that, I never heard from her again. In the early seventies I had a dream where I was looking at a photo album with a group of people. They were mostly pictures of places I had visited. Then there was a picture of three women. Someone pointed to one of them and said to me, 'Is this your mother?'

"I said, 'No, she is not in the picture.' From that I knew she was no longer alive. I have put her in the Light many times, particularly after I knew she had passed on, and I just say, 'Stay in the Light. Accept it, so that you will understand your life better, so that you can really walk fully in the Light,' and I let these thoughts spin around her as I remember her."

On my way home that night I started to think about my own mother in the spirit of forgiveness that Swami Radha had described. She had been an extremely critical person, or so it seemed to me since I had often been the subject of her scathing anger. On the other hand, she was a passionate, intelligent woman and I knew in spite of my opposition to her that I loved and respected her. Now Swami Radha had given me a way to think about my mother's life compassionately, with a desire to understand rather than get even. So I started and pretty soon I was thinking about her as a flesh and blood human being, someone just like myself who must have had dreams for a full and happy life. The sadness is that she traded those dreams, which were reflections of her deepest convictions, for the romantic dream of a perfect marriage and happiness ever after.

The day Canada officially entered the war against Germany in 1939, my mother left the hospital in downtown Toronto where she worked as a registered nurse and went around the corner to the Canadian Army recruiting office on Dupont Street, where she applied to join the army medical corp. That night my father, to whom she was then engaged, hit the roof.

"If you go," he said, "you may as well forget about any wedding."

My mother was a spirited woman but she was also drawn to the security that marriage implied in those days. She tore up the application and that was the end of it.

Although she never admitted it, I think the compromise my mother made for the sake of marriage dealt her spirit a blow from which it never really recovered. I come to this conclusion only through my observations of her while I was growing up. My mother didn't reveal much of herself but now and then she would tell me little anecdotes of her life before she married. Sometimes I could detect a tone in her voice, something that made me wonder what she was really thinking as she told her story. I wondered what her life would have been like had she been willing or able to follow her most spirited impulses. Her early pursuits suggest that it would have been very different.

In 1932, the year of her high school graduation, my mother applied and was accepted into nursing school at the Toronto General Hospital, starting that fall.

By the time she married at the age of twenty-five, her nursing career included special training under the direction of the noted Montreal brain surgeon, Wilder Penfield, as well as three months in the burn ward at New York's Long Island General Hospital, where she studied advanced therapeutic techniques for the treatment of burn victims. Her training was severely tested on the afternoon the German dirigible, Hindenburg, exploded over New Jersey while attempting to land.

Although there were surprisingly few fatalities, several passengers and hundreds of spectators below got caught in the burning debris and suffered terrible burns. Long Island Hospital was closest to the scene of the tragedy and soon filled to capacity. My mother said that her team worked almost seventy-two hours looking after victims of the accident, with time out only for quick meals and a few brief hours of sleep between shifts. With her experience and specialized training, she was a prime candidate for immediate acceptance into the army medical corp. But in the end she turned it down.

In my mother's day few options outside marriage and family were considered worthwhile or even respectable for a young woman to pursue. The war changed that view dramatically, though temporarily. Thousands of women enlisted in the armed services. Many more went into the factories and onto the land to keep life going while the men formerly employed in these industries crossed the oceans to wage war. Yet no matter how compelling my mother's dreams may have been at the time, they were not powerful enough to overcome her need for a man's acceptance. Thinking it through, taking time to put together a larger picture of who my mother had been, my heart started to fill with gratitude for her. That was the beginning of the healing between us.

A few years ago Swami Radha told me about a practice I could do using the Divine Mother prayer from the *Ananda Lahari* (Wave of Bliss), a fifteenth-century sacred poem celebrating the power of Creation in the feminine form. Swami Radha's practice consisted of repeating the Divine Mother prayer twenty-five times at the end of her regular daily mantra chanting.

"But you don't just repeat it," she said, reminding me of her own guru's insistence that she must never let the recitation of mantra become mechanical. "Bring all your focus and concentration into each line. Make the prayer an offering. Use your emotions for that," she said, concluding her description of what was needed to make the practice real.

The rest she was leaving up to me.

Something about the prayer made me decide to try the practice for three months as part of a focused effort to combat my arrogance, particularly the intellectual male arrogance that was seriously affecting how I related to women. I went into the practice with two compatible goals in mind: the first was to transform my arrogance through listening; the second was to make peace with the feminine in myself, whatever that meant.

The first morning I went to do the practice in the old beach prayer room below Main House, the weather was gray and sodden with wet snow and freezing rain. For the next three months, at the same time each morning, I would go to the prayer room and chant the mantra for two hours followed by twenty-five recitations of the Divine Mother prayer, all counted out on the beads of my mala. Even though I resisted the practice, the damp, overcast mornings that winter made the silent, embracing warmth of the prayer room a pleasant place to be so early in the day. At times, the warmth was the only thing keeping me there.

The Divine Mother prayer started acting immediately, though in ways that I would not have expected. Each morning I would start by chanting the mantra, Hari Om, and before long I'd be off somewhere in strange fields of sexual fantasy involving the Tibetan Buddhist image of Tara. In order to bring focus and control back into the practice, I would chant a little harder while berating myself for turning a spiritual practice into self-indulgent gratification. All this did was intensify the fantasies and spin me around faster.

One morning the vibration of the mantra penetrated my resistance and self-will. This was my first experience of listening in a different way. Gradually the vibration filled my upper chest and shoulders, then overflowed into the room. The softening deepened, the fantasies disappeared, and I was filled with a wonderful, expansive feeling of gratitude. From then on few fantasies of any kind appeared during the morning chanting, but the feeling of gratitude came back over and over again.

The sexual connection to the image of Tara, which had been disconcerting, now made sense. My experience with Tara as an ideal had shown me what happens when the power of a mantra is used to raise the sexual experience from its usual level of physical-emotional gratification to the level of finer feelings—the heart. When I wrote a paper for Swami Radha describing this experience with the Divine Mother prayer, she expanded on it and presented me with a new challenge.

"Sometimes, David, what you have interpreted as sexual feelings arising in your mantra practice may not be that at all. The feelings can start in the area of the genitals, that is true. But if you allow it those feelings can also expand upwards in a spiral movement, producing waves of experience a thousand times greater than the procreation level of sexual orgasm. This can happen between two people without even touching each other. The currents pass from one to the other like waves of an electric line in parallel. Only when this happens is it possible to understand what true sharing is, what true giving is. But you don't need another person to experience this. You need first to understand it as the interaction of purusha and prakriti* within yourself. After you have done the initial work on yourself and have learned to control your mind and emotions, you can ask Divine Mother to reveal something more of Herself. You realize that you need Her to manifest the rest. Then you just wait and see what happens. It can be very strengthening. So keep on going with what you're doing. Om Om."

Swami Radha brought her hands together at her heart, then reached up and gave me a hug. In that moment there was tremendous power in the warmth of her love.

I did keep on, and one morning about two and a half months into the Divine Mother practice, the floodgates suddenly opened. On the third or fourth repetition of the prayer, I suddenly broke down and cried as I never have cried before—deep, deep sobbing that seemed to come from some place far away, wave after wave of tears overflowing into the prayer room. It was so startling and came from such a deep place that in the midst of it all I started to worry about what was hap-

---

* Spirit and matter; male and female; the Unseen and the Seen.

pening to me. Where was all this coming from? Then I cried out, "I'm sorry, I'm sorry, I'm sorry," with such intense feeling that you would have thought I had just unearthed some unspeakable memory from the past, something so terrible that it could only be revealed in this way. But there was no tangible memory. I had no idea what was at the root of this spontaneous and deep sorrow except that, whatever it was, I clearly needed to balance the record. Of this I was certain.

Swami Radha put this into perspective for me when she said, "What greater act of love could there be than to provide the opportunity over and over for undoing the mistakes of the past in order to take the next step toward Higher Consciousness, towards the Light? It is the Mother who gave you this opportunity and it is through the Mother that you can redeem yourself if you are willing to listen."

Her own guru, Swami Sivananda, had said to her in India on the day of her mantra initiation, "Be a spiritual mother to all. The son or daughter who has been truant will always go back to the mother first."

My experience of the Divine Mother prayer told me this was true. If Divine Mother is all of life itself, all the energy there is, then the quickest way to liberation has to be through the day-to-day experience of life itself, transforming the illusions and disappointments, the shortcomings and strengths, the insights and the victories, into wisdom and compassion. Through the Divine Mother prayer, I had finally understood that freedom starts with forgiveness and personal responsibility.

O Divine Mother
May all my speech and idle talk be mantra
All actions of my hands be mudra
All eating and drinking
be the offering of oblations unto Thee
All lying down, prostrations before Thee
May all pleasures be as dedicating
my entire self unto Thee
May everything I do be taken as Thy worship.

CHAPTER SEVENTEEN

Temple of Light

S wami Radha is gazing softly into the goldfish pond in her garden in front of Many Mansions. She holds her hands clasped
behind her as she rocks ever so gently back and forth. The evening air
is soft and warm; the sun is just starting to disappear behind the mountains
on the other side of the lake.

"I think it went pretty well," she says. "The temple looks just great."

She is referring to the weekend celebration dedicating the new Temple of
Divine Light at the ashram on that warm July day in 1992.

I nod silently and look up at the temple's soaring white arches against the
azure sky. I wonder what thoughts have gone through her mind on this very
special day, sixty-five years after she first dreamed of the temple as a young
girl in Germany. For many years she had all but given up hope that the
temple would be built in her lifetime. And yet here it is.

~

On separate occasions in the early sixties, Swami Radha met two women
who were psychic.

One said to her, "You built a temple long ago. Then it was square
and filled with light. This time your work will be completed and the
temple will be round."

The other woman told her that the temple would not be built until
everyone in the ashram was in harmony with her.

"That could take many years," she said, assessing the situation clearly.

When the foundation for the temple was built in 1965, everyone in the ashram was confident that the next stage, the temple building itself, would soon follow; it was just a matter of raising the money needed to build it. That was the feeling, but it didn't turn out that way. When the money failed to appear and the residents turned their attention to other work in the ashram, Swami Radha accepted the likelihood that the temple would not be built for some time. Twenty years later when there was still no one willing to take on the project, Swami Radha concluded that the temple would not be built during her lifetime.

Then in September 1988, Swami Radha almost died. To this day I don't know what her illness was, although I expect it was related to her arthritis. The facts are that she became so ill one night that she had to be rushed to hospital in Nelson, and had that not happened it is most likely she would not have lasted the night. That's how close it was and it scared me a lot. None of us were prepared for her to go yet.

Her Divine Committee must have thought the same because within a few days of entering hospital, she regained enough strength to start organizing a trip to the Radha House in Victoria where she planned to convalesce over the winter. When I went to see her in hospital it was obvious that she had done some very strong soul-searching about the remainder of her life, specifically what she was still being asked to do. The temple was foremost on her mind when I stood at the foot of her bed on the day she was supposed to leave for Victoria. While others in the room continued packing for the trip, Swami Radha gave me her instructions. Although she was weak and her voice sounded strained, she was absolutely unequivocal about what she wanted me to do. After she finished speaking there was no question in my mind either.

"I want you to build the temple," she said. "It has gone on long enough now and it must be finished. There is an architect here in Nelson, I met his wife a long time ago—a very fine person—and she said her husband can't get the right kind of work. He is very good.... Anyway, find out. Get something going and keep me informed. You can phone me anytime, or fax. I am asking you to do this, David, because I think you are the one meant to do it. Hari Om."

On the way back to the ashram, my head spun under the weight of her request. The most complex structure I had ever built on my own was the equipment shed addition to the ashram barn. I didn't feel even remotely qualified to build a temple even though I had promised Swami Radha I would. Then two weeks after my meeting with her in the hospital, a remarkable little event showed me that I would not be doing it alone.

Mr. Temple wasn't his real name but it suits the role he played early on in the project. In fact he was a retired Ukrainian carpenter living in Creston, a small rural community about eighty kilometers south of the ashram. My first encounter with Mr. Temple happened at the Canada-U. S. border crossing south of Creston just a couple of days after I had made contact with the Nelson architect. I was in the customs office on the Canadian side looking after some business for the ashram when an enormous old maroon-colored Chrysler pulled up outside driven by an elderly man who could barely see over the steering wheel.

The old man rolled down the window and called out to the border guard, "You want to see in the trunk, see all the stuff I'm sneaking in, eh?"

The guard's jocular response told me that the two of them had probably bantered back and forth like this countless times, but he went outside to look anyway just to play along. As the old man got out of his car to open the trunk, I noticed a sheet of paper slide off the driver's seat onto the road beneath the car door. Thinking that he might not have seen it, I went outside to pick it up for him. It was a photocopy of a beautiful domed church, octagonal in shape, almost identical to Swami Radha's dream temple without the soaring arches. I was stunned. The expression on my face must have caught the old man's attention.

"You like?" he asked, not waiting for a reply. "My son, he send it to me from the Arctic. They build that church there in Inuvik. You know where that is? Cold there, eh!"

I just listened and nodded, not quite believing what was happening. The old man grinned, happy maybe to have someone who was actually interested in what he had to say. Boy, was I ever.

"Anyway, he knows I would like to see that. I build lots of dome churches in my time. Ukrainian churches," he laughed, "and my son, lots of times he come and help me on the job."

I told him about the proposed temple at Kootenay Bay.

"I come see you some time," he said. "See what you got going there."

And with that he got back into the old maroon Chrysler, waved to the border guard and drove away. The guard turned to me and started to laugh.

"Nuttier than a fruit cake," he said. "But I hear he was one helluva good carpenter."

Two days later I got a call from the ashram office saying there was someone here to see me.

"He's here about the temple. Says you know all about it."

I walked up toward the office and sure enough the big old Chrysler was there in the parking lot.

When Mr. Temple saw the foundation for the building he grew quiet and thoughtful, then got up on the foundation platform and started walking around it, stopping every few steps to look closely at how it was put together. All the time he was muttering to himself and occasionally he would stop and look at me, shake his head, then continue walking. When he jumped off the platform and walked down the side of the hill around to the lake side, he began to speak in a very excited manner.

"You must build this," he said. "This is history. See down here where we walked, you see? Make stone steps just like Egypt. Yes, yes. Must build. History. Very important, you understand?"

Before Mr. Temple left that morning, he gave me an architect's plan of a Ukrainian Church he had built just outside Edmonton almost twenty years ago. The drawing showed a domed, eight-sided cupola at the center of the church.

I was to see Mr. Temple two more times at the border crossing within the next four months. In the meantime I left instructions with the Nelson architect to have conceptual drawings of the temple ready for the ashram's annual general meeting, which was scheduled for two days between Christmas and New Year's. A week before Christmas I happened to meet Mr. Temple on the main street in Creston.

"How's it going there?" he asked right away, meaning the temple, of course.

"Good," I said. "The architect will have drawings ready for us between Christmas and New Year's."

"Tell him three windows," said Mr. Temple, holding up three fingers. "Make them round at the top—like those over there."

He pointed to a store window across the street.

"Each side of the octagon should have three windows."

Mr. Temple gazed at me intently, nodding his head. Then he laughed and put out his hand.

"Merry Christmas!" he said.

We shook hands and he walked up the street. I looked again at the three arched windows in the store across the street and again I didn't know what to think. Mr. Temple had never seen our drawings, nor had I told him anything about windows. Yet the three arched windows in each facet of the octagon was exactly how Swami Radha had seen it in her dream sixty-five years ago. When I called to tell her about this latest contact with Mr. Temple, she laughed delightedly. But she didn't say anything more about it.

"I have good news," she said. "The doctor says I am doing great. All the tests are coming out okay. He thinks it will be fine for me to come back to the ashram this spring."

That was good news to me. She would be here for the start-up of the temple construction.

Nine months after that, around the middle of August, Mr. Temple again paid a visit to the ashram. By this time the foundation had been rebuilt, the walls were framed up, and the work was moving along well. But something in Mr. Temple had changed. He seemed cranky and bad-tempered, barely even acknowledging me as he walked around the building site.

"Why you doing that?" he growled, pointing to one of the framed walls. "Why you bothering to do this? No good. Tear it all down. You can't build on old foundation. Nothing will work."

And so forth along these lines until I just didn't want to hear any more. When Mr. Temple had finished criticizing everything he could think of, he left without saying goodbye. I stood at the temple entrance feeling heavy and disappointed as I watched him walk down the road. Ted Wallace, one of the professional builders on the job, came over and asked me who the old guy was.

"I don't know," I said. "He came here once before and he was very different then, really supportive and excited. But now it's all different. I don't know what's going on with him."

Ted picked up his saw and laughed.

"Rude old crock," he said.

That night I told Swami Radha about the strange visit.

"It's almost as if he had a completely different mind," I said to her.

"He probably did," she replied, in a matter-of-fact tone.

By the end of our first year on the project, we had the temple up, closed in, and the roof on before the first serious snowfall. It was an exhilarating finish to a year that had demanded a lot from everyone living in the ashram who directly or indirectly supported the project. We set a date for start-up in the spring with our two full-time contractors, and broke for Christmas. I was physically exhausted and ready for a couple of months away from the building.

Unfortunately it turned out to be more than a couple of months. One afternoon in early spring just after we started work again, I was climbing a scaffold that we'd erected in the center of the building to reach the ceiling, when I missed a rung and fell eighteen feet to the floor. Two things stay clearly in my mind from that frozen instant between missing the rung and hitting the floor. The first is the rush of terror through my heart as I reached out and grabbed nothing but air. The second was a crystal-clear insight that came to me as I twisted through the air: if I could just keep moving after I hit the floor I would be all right. I even said it out loud...just keep moving...as a tremendous crash resounded through the empty temple. After that, nothing. The pain shooting up my back and through my left shoulder made it certain that I wasn't going anywhere. My job supervising the construction of Swami Radha's temple had just come to an end.

The first stages of remorse and self-pity (it was hard to tell which) came over me on the Sunday afternoon three days after the orthopedic surgery to rebuild my left arm. I had been a good patient until then—cooperative, pleasant, suffering nobly while making absolutely no demands on a nursing staff that was over-worked and under-appreciated. By Sunday, however, I gave up the charade and became normal which, given the amount of pain I was in, meant demanding and obnoxious. The nurse on duty responded to my pleas for relief with apparent indifference. She is ignoring me, I said to myself. She is cold and indifferent and utterly lacking in compassion, I added when she brought just two aspirins. I feel really terrible, was the truth I reached before giving up. She appeared a moment or two later standing by the side of my bed and looking at me closely with great compassion in her eyes. I was sobbing deeply.

"Do you see?" I cried. "Do you see what pride can do? This is what pride does."

She didn't say anything. She just took my hand and held it until I calmed down and started to fall asleep. I didn't even hear her leave.

Looking back at this now, I recognize that healing began for me when pride could no longer deny the fact of the accident or what I had done to contribute to it. But it was healing on a much more substantial level than just the physical body. That night in the hospital I had a dream about the road drawing from the Music and Consciousness workshop in Sioux Lookout ten years earlier. In the dream the huge black boulder that had blocked the road was now split into two equal halves that had each rolled off the road and into the ditch on either side. From the center of the broken halves came a faint but steady emanation of rose-colored light. I awakened from that dream feeling better than I had in a long, long time.

Gradually my body began to reflect the healing that was taking place in my mind and heart. A couple of months after I got home from the hospital, I signed up for a three-week certification course in Swami Radha's Hidden Language Hatha Yoga®, an approach that restores Hatha yoga to the Kundalini system of Higher Consciousness. Hidden Language is the only truly reflective method of Hatha Yoga taught in the world today.

I wasn't thinking so highly of it by the end of the first day of the course. The pain was so intense—especially in my lower back where one of the vertebrae had fractured in the accident—that I was more than ready to reconsider my decision to take the course. However, when I awoke the next morning, there was no pain. For the first time since the accident I awoke without pain. This pattern continued over the next three weeks with diminishing bouts of pain each day. By the middle of the third week I did salamba sirshasana, the shoulder stand, on my own after a nudge of encouragement from the instructor had tweaked my pride in just the right way.

"You can do it," she had said, with just a hint of challenge in her voice. "Just try."

I was so piqued by her presumptuous tone that I immediately closed my eyes, gritted my teeth and hoisted myself up into the shoulder stand. The pain was excruciating. In seconds I was soaked with sweat. But it worked. I went past a threshold of pain that had been imposed by an artificial barrier, just like a certain boulder in the road I had known about for years. That was an important breakthrough for me.

And so my experience with the Temple of Divine Light came to a close. In time I was able to work on it again but I never went back to the old way of working—the controlling, hard-driving, no-room-for-others way. That way no longer had a place in the ashram. For a long time I kept on my altar a reflection on matsyasana, the fish pose, that I had written during the hatha course. It was a good reminder of what pride and resistance had cost.

Some fish will go down to the bottom of the sea, there to burrow into the mud and darkness. They do this to hide, to avoid danger, or to look for food. I am doing the same. For a long time I was close to the surface, highly visible, agile, flexible—sometimes too clever for my own good— taking my cues from what I could see. Now I am trying to go deeper into the darkness. I know that to remain on the surface means certain death.

The bottom of the sea where the light cannot go is the deepest recess of my unconscious mind. There I shall find the food for my redemption. When the fish is caught it struggles violently to get away. I think about being hooked by the Divine and how much I have struggled to get away. Can I allow myself to go into the Divine Fisher's boat, to be taken to the other shore? That is the question I cannot yet answer.

CHAPTER EIGHTEEN

Next Step

The day after Christmas, 1988, I made a quick trip to Calgary to pick up Swami Radha and bring her back for the ashram's annual general meeting. She had been staying at the Radha House in Calgary for several months. At supper the night I arrived she presented me with a small, carefully wrapped box—my Christmas present—and she seemed eager that I open it right away. Inside was a man's black onyx ring with two little diamonds on either side of the oval stone, all set in shining gold. I didn't know what to say. The only other ring I had ever been given was my wedding ring, which I suddenly became very conscious of on my left hand. I slipped the new ring onto the ring finger of my right hand and turned it slowly under the light. It was elegant and unassuming, so much like Swami Radha, and the beautiful black onyx appeared to float in the soft, golden light.

According to the legends, black is Radha's favorite color. Although Radha longed for Krishna, even had visions of him, she could never know all of him and the color black represents that unknown. We can never know all of that divine power that has created us and sustained us and will one day take us back again. I have a picture of Krishna wearing a ring very similar to the one Swami Radha gave me.

Swami Radha placed great value on the symbolic meaning of jewelry, particularly since it had often appeared in her dreams right from early childhood. I knew this, and gratefully accepted the gift, knowing that it contained a message for me. I didn't know what that message was, but coming from her, it was clear that I was precious in her eyes. I knew the gift was more than it appeared to be.

We talked, then, about what it means to be Krishna's friend. Swami Radha described it as being able to respond with sensitivity to other people and what they need, accepting their weaknesses, serving them, and allowing them to keep their integrity. That night I wrote in my diary that this kind of service and attitude is what true spiritual life is about. Spiritual life is not about walking around acting holy and saying the right things. Spiritual life means ongoing surrender of self-will and self-expression—my way, and only my way—in order to see and hear what is needed, in order to hear the flute. Swami Radha's gift encouraged me to keep moving forward. When I finished writing that night, I slipped the black onyx ring onto my wedding finger to see if it fit. It did, but I wasn't quite ready to leave it there yet.

My paper on marriage and spiritual life written at such an early stage in my understanding nevertheless showed clearly that I understood more about renunciation than letting go of a few basic possessions. The understanding was there but the willingness had been slow to follow. Lately, the spirit of renunciation which I viewed as a particular kind of intelligence had again been calling me to loosen my hold on the two people I had loved most of all in my life. Yet it was obvious to me that renunciation as a spiritual ideal could hardly be realized by turning my back on my former commitments. Even if I had thought that was possible, Swami Radha wouldn't have allowed it for a minute.

The fact was Donna and I were getting ready to take the next step. We had both received a mantra initiation from Swami Radha, Alicia was in her last year of high school, and as Swami Radha had said at our Rose Ceremony, "When the time is right we'll take the next step." The time was getting to be right; I knew that much anyway. It was more a question of knowing what that step would be for each of us, either individually or together. Until the morning Donna asked to speak to me about "something important" on her mind, I didn't know what that step was going to be.

She seemed upset when we sat down to talk and it took a few minutes to find out what was happening. A lot. My wife, my travel companion for many years, told me in a voice shaking with emotion that she was ready to take an initiation into sanyas. When I asked her how she knew, she opened her diary to a dream she'd had in the previous week which made it clear where her heart and mind were. She said that an intense mantra practice she had just completed was pointing to the same thing. For several weeks she had tried to ignore the signs that were telling her it was time to take this next step along the path of renunciation. Now she could no longer do that.

In the spirit that had brought us onto the spiritual path, I embraced my wife and told her that I would fully support her. In my heart I felt that was true. Our life together had been sustained by this fundamental principle—that we would support each other's spiritual growth as long as it was not at the cost of injury to the other. In light of her dreams and my response, Donna immediately wrote to Swami Radha about her intentions. That night Swami Radha called the three of us over to Many Mansions.

It was Alicia who broached the subject immediately.

"I want to know what the relationship between my mom and dad will be," she asked Swami Radha as soon as we were together in the sunroom.

"After your mother has sanyas? Not much different from what it is now. The only difference is that your mother will stay a little more focused on the sanyas. It's the same as if she was wanting to learn another language, Spanish, say. She would need to stay focused as much as she could in order to do that.

"But there are other considerations. Let's say the wife is wanting to take sanyas. Her husband can become very proud and say, 'I am the better one, you know.' Then there will be competition and jealousy between them. But with a different attitude the husband can say, 'That I have such a wife is a special grace and I will do anything to make her life easier.' Now that would be a very different response.

"Anandamayi Ma was still quite young, in her early thirties, when she approached her husband and said, 'I can't be your wife anymore.' The reason was this great spiritual longing she had that made it impossible for her to focus on her husband. You know what he told her? He said, 'Then I will be your first disciple, and I will be the first one to serve you.'

"I think for any man there can be no greater grace than to have a wife like that. Under different circumstances a woman can ruin man's life, a man's business, his career, she can even destroy his honor. But she can also be a tremendous blessing, as this example of Anandamayi Ma makes clear. But it's only a male who is aware and conscious of the course of evolution, who has made the effort to get his instincts under control and realize what his true potential is, who will form a friendship with the woman who has an intense spiritual longing."

Swami Radha paused and smiled at Alicia.

"What do you have on your ankle? Is it a cord?"

"It's like embroidery threads made into an ankle bracelet."

"Oh, embroidery thread. Well, in my time we had a little gold chain. And if a young woman had already set the date then she would put a tiny little medallion on the chain where it joins together. That was a sign for other men to stay away. She was already signed up!" Swami Radha laughed. "You see? It all comes back. Of course!"

We sat for a few minutes not saying anything. I was happy that we were able to enter this next step together with Swami Radha because truthfully I didn't have a clue what would happen to our marriage after Donna's initiation. That night she explained to us that having chosen the path of renunciation implies the right to go as far in this life as we wish towards the goal of Liberation and Higher Consciousness. Using the example of marriage, Swami Radha said that for a couple to evolve spiritually, a change in the relationship is needed.

"Samadhi—the state of spiritual self-consciousness or enlightened self-realization—has six stages," she said, "and probably many more after that. Even the first is very difficult to attain, mainly because of the power of attachment. Attachment is a serious barrier to awareness."

In the past Swami Radha had cautioned my tendency to put on a brave face in order to hide what I really felt and with this situation I was trying not to do that. Yet to me the initiation obviously had serious implications for our marriage. I thought sanyas would probably end it but Swami Radha saw it differently.

"Just the opposite," she said. "The decision to take sanyas will never end a marriage. On the other hand, if you were to go looking for a pretty face in the ashram and start following that around, then the marriage would end very fast. If you were that type of a man, having a wife who is a sanyasin would pretty much keep you from mischief, you see? That is one thing.

"But actually I have already seen the desire both of you had for spiritual life in your Music and Consciousness workshop. Do you remember when we put your drawings side by side on the floor? Now it sounds pretty tough what I am saying here, but it was evident in the workshop that your marriage would eventually have broken up because the marriage in a traditional sense had nothing more to offer. You had nothing more to give to her, and she didn't have much more to give you, which is how marriages end. But what the workshop helped you to see was that you both had high spiritual inclinations and that you really ought to work together as a team. From what I have seen marriage makes sense only if a man and woman want to bring out the best in each other, as you're attempting to do here today. If that desire in each of you is strong enough then I don't see why you both couldn't become sanyasins if you wanted to.

"How you and Donna go about things is between yourselves and God. But it will help you to remember that the instincts will always want to overrule the Divine. Forces opposed to the Light are constantly interacting with your ideals. They must become known and seen at all times. In a spiritual marriage you become aware of sexual energy and its many diverse forms. Don't tempt God. When the male and female qualities in yourselves are married, balance is achieved, and you will

see that there will not be too much emotion or too much intellect coming between you. As Jesus said, 'In the will of God you are free.' In
other words, renunciation means to be acting in the will of God. Your
spiritual life must become your new love affair and the love must be
kept alive so that the affair is ongoing."

Donna was initiated into sanyas on a cold, windy, overcast day in
January of 1989, several months after our evening with Swami Radha.
Only sanyasins could attend the mid-afternoon ceremony at Many
Mansions, which was fine with me until about an hour before the ceremony was supposed to start. Until then I had been a model husband
and true friend to my wife, encouraging her every step of the way.
Once she left the house to get ready for the ceremony, I collapsed into
despair. After a few minutes of feeling awful, the complete reverse came
over me and I felt positively elated. Then back to despair. So it went for
the next two hours, back and forth between these two emotional ex-
tremes, until somewhere in between them I suddenly had the insight
that neither one was real.

"Neither is real," I cried out, "therefore something else must be,
something that is true."

This insight produced a remarkably peaceful feeling that stayed with
me for the rest of the afternoon.

But it took time to accept the change, particularly a few months
later after Donna (now Swami Radhakrishnananda) moved to Toronto
to help out with the work there for an indefinite period of time. Perhaps it was divinely ordained in some ways, but the day she was leaving I happened to be conducting a spiritual retreat for men in the ashram.
After lunch I was in my room when I heard a knock on the door.

"I've come to say goodbye," she said.

Without saying anything, I took her in my arms and held her. Neither of us could speak. We just stood there clinging to each other.
Finally she had to go. At the door she turned and looked at me.

"I'll meet you in the Light," she said. "I promise. I'll meet you in the
Light."

Then she was gone.

Those were dark days in the months that followed as my lesser self despaired at what it perceived as the end of a friendship. For a long time it felt as if the purpose for doing anything had simply vanished. What was the point? When Swami Radha asked me to take on the building of the temple I turned to work, as I had often done in the past, pouring the loneliness into a drive for perfection. And of course that was not the way to approach either the building or the resolution of my emotions. The fall from the scaffold, when it came, put an end to both. Only then could the real healing begin.

~

Although I tried hard to deny it, my wife's decision to take sanyas had forced me to look at where I was on the path and what my next step was going to be. Now that I was in effect single again, would I follow suit and take an initiation into sanyas too, or would I follow other inclinations? I had enough sense to know that nothing of the familiar would remain. And that was the problem. For several months following Donna's initiation I was continually at sea, caught in an emotional turmoil that was driven by deep sadness and loneliness. Such was the power of these emotions that they caused me to forget the friendship we had developed together, and to diminish all that Swami Radha and the ashram had come to mean to me. It was as if a huge portion of my life had simply vanished.

Emotional dependency was the issue. Who am I without my wife and family? What possible worth do I have now that they no longer need me? Emotional dependency created questions that had no real answers; emotional dependency thrived on the premise that I had no intrinsic worth on my own; emotional dependency is the root of attachment and was therefore the cause of my suffering. Why on earth would I want to be emotionally dependent on anyone? Because without knowing it, emotional dependency was what I had called love, even experienced as love within the limitations of my understanding.

Pain, I was beginning to learn, could be a great teacher.

And so I had to wait to see if sanyas was an option for me. Wait and let the idea go, and in the meantime bring my focus back to my spiritual practices and reflection. My spiritual objective during this difficult time was to bring more of the feminine out in myself, particularly in my interactions with others, and to learn how to become my own best friend. Gradually the practices took hold, first on a level so subtle that most of the time I was unaware of anything changing, then becoming palpable enough that I could feel a response coming back from the people around me, but starting from somewhere deep within myself. The Light was beginning to take the form of self-acceptance and gratitude, and I started to reach out to others once again.

Finally, a little over a year after Donna's initiation, I took the opportunity of a rose ceremony that is offered in the ashram every spring. Using the petals of a rose I offered each one to the water with the prayer that Divine Mother accept all that I am, all that I have been, in Her service. This offering I made from the heart in a way that I had not experienced before. Perhaps it was surrender, a response from another part of myself that knew exactly why it was here on this path, going through these fiery tests. I needed to take a stand for my own potential.

Half an hour after the ceremony, my rusty armor of masculine pride crashed to the kitchen floor in Main House under the scathing response of a very angry woman who was clearly unhappy with something I had said. She was upset by the arrogance in my tone of voice which, she said, diminished her and made her feel stupid. I was stunned, but for the first time I also heard the tone in my voice that had caused such anguish. As if in response to my offering in the rose ceremony, Divine Mother rushed in to show me the unfinished business that needed still to be dealt with if I was truly to become her servant.

Later that summer I was working in the recording studio at Many Mansions one afternoon when Swami Radha came in. I was editing some tape while listening through a headset and I hadn't heard her enter. Suddenly, very softly, she covered my eyes with her hands from behind. Of course I knew whose hands they were and I reached up and took them in my own, turning around in the chair to look at her. She was laughing quietly at her little game and for a moment the closeness between us was indescribably sweet as I continued to hold her hands in mine.

"So," she said, "have you been thinking about sanyas?"

"Yes," I said, surprised at hearing myself say it.

"And do you know what name you would take?" she asked.

"Yes," I said, again with a confidence and knowing that surprised me. "Gopalananda."

Gopalananda, the youthful Krishna, the mischievous one, stealer of butter and gopi's hearts.

"The name suits you," she laughed. "I think that's it all right."

～

In September 1991, I was initiated into sanyas and given the name Gopalananda—*Gopala* the youthful Krishna, plus *ananda* meaning bliss. The potential inherent in the name wasn't likely to manifest any too soon, I thought, but I was at least aware of it. Spiritual babies, like regular babies, have to grow into their potential and I was happy just to be taking another step towards my own. All that remained was to find something appropriate to give to Swami Radha in gratitude for what she had given me. The problem was that I didn't own anything of value apart from an antique wedding ring that I had thought would one day go to Alicia.

The ring, a platinum and silver filigree with a small cluster of diamonds gathered around a large solitaire, had been given to me by my grandmother a week before she died. It had been her mother's wedding ring. Until my initiation into sanyas, it had never occurred to me to sell it. Now, in spite of my vow of renunciation, I still felt a responsibility towards Alicia even though she had done well on her own for several years. With these thoughts rolling around in my mind, I decided to sell the ring and send Alicia the money.

A week later the jeweler who had appraised the ring phoned.

"I have someone here who is interested in buying the ring," he said. "If you want to bring it back I can sell it for you this afternoon."

The figure he mentioned was more money than I had seen in years, a veritable godsend and I would have said yes immediately if it hadn't been for the voice that suddenly came out of nowhere.

"Give the ring to Swami Radha."

"No. I can't."

"Give the ring to Swami Radha."

"No. Don't you see? I have to help my daughter."

Silence. Long pause. I thought it best not to say anything more to the jeweler. And of course the next morning I knew what I had to do. As soon as I affirmed it to myself a feeling of elation came over me. I put the ring back in its little box and after a quick breakfast went to see Swami Radha at Many Mansions.

She looked at the ring for a long time without saying a word. Then she looked up at me, then back to the ring.

"It belonged to your grandmother?"

"Yes. But I've had it for years."

"I see," she nodded. "It is very beautiful. Thank you."

And that was it. The ring had found its rightful place. I had no idea then, and didn't find out until several years later, that the ring had confirmed one of her most extraordinary dreams about Lord Krishna— a wedding dream in which they were married.

A week after my initiation into sanyas I had a dream that confirmed my own direction.

Donna and I are walking alongside a railway track in the Simla foot-hills of India. The terrain slopes gently upward towards the hills in the distance. She is walking in front of me, I am behind. We are both dressed in the ochre cloth of sanyasins. A train comes along behind us. Because of the incline, it has slowed almost to a walking pace. A beautiful old steam engine, fully restored and painted in black with dark green and red accents at the front, pulls a long string of flatcars. The sun is high in the sky and the air is crystal clear.

Donna reaches up to a steel ladder on the side of one of the flatcars as it goes by. She gracefully pulls herself up the ladder and onto the deck where there are rows of seats just like a regular passenger train, only set up in the open air. Most of the seats are occupied, a few are still vacant. Donna goes directly to an empty seat and sits down.

In the meantime, after I have seen her climb the ladder at the front of the car, I turn and grab the ladder at the rear of the car just as it is going by. The train is moving so slowly at this point, it is easy to climb aboard. However, when I get to the deck instead of going directly to the empty seat beside Donna, I stop and say hello to everyone, being very cheerful, friendly, passing the time of day as I slowly make my way towards the front of the car.

I awoke from this dream laughing out loud after seeing one of my more prominent personalities acting out so true to character. I laughed, but I was grateful for the confirmation too. The dream also demonstrated rather graphically that the initiation ceremony itself had not been sufficient to dissolve old personality aspects into the ocean of faded memories. One personality aspect simply dons the new garb and carries on as usual, a response that underscores one of the most important aspects of the spiritual path. I could see that what I brought with me from the past was what I had to work with on the path. My mantra initiation and vow of renunciation was meant to be used to bring all aspects of my life together, not drive them apart.

Just how much my friendly wandering mind affected my ability to focus and concentrate, particularly around Swami Radha, became a real issue several months after my initiation when I helped her move from the Radha House in Victoria to the new Radha House in Vancouver. Part of my job was to help set up the house according to what she needed, which meant doing everything from unpacking boxes of books to wiring in new lights and even hanging a mirror in her bedroom. It was the mirror that did me in.

"Where is your mind?" she asked, her voice cracking under the strain of accumulated frustration.

We were standing together in her room looking at our reflection in the mirror I had just hung on the wall over her dresser. It was perfect. The mirror was at exactly the right height—for me. For her, the mirror would work only if she stood on her toes. As it was she could see only the top of her head.

I looked into the mirror as steadily as I could.

"Swami Radha," I said, "I don't know where my mind is. I haven't a clue where it's gone."

She looked at me for a moment, then shook her head and turned away. At some point during the week, I couldn't say exactly when, my mind had wandered away from the job I was here to do and the minimal attention I was bringing to her needs hadn't been enough to carry out even the simplest of her requests. It was the most powerful expression of stubborn resistance I had ever experienced. The evidence was standing right in front of me, right before my eyes.

Swami Radha appeared relieved when I told her I had to leave the next day to go back to the ashram. I was relieved too.

It was true what she had often said to me, "On the spiritual path a wandering mind is a dangerous thing. You never know where it will take you or where you'll end up. It may not be where you would ever want to go, and sometimes it is extremely difficult finding your way back."

Siva, the Destroyer of Obstacles, entered my heart and began His work. One look at Shakti Dakini in the first chakra of the Kundalini system* and I just knew that she could dispel arrogance with a single sidelong glance, like lightning cracking apart the blackness on a stormy night. Among her formidable weapons, Shakti Dakini held a simple wooden bowl, empty and ready to be filled with...what? Maybe the fruits of surrender. If I accept her and surrender to her (drink from her

---

* See Swami Sivananda Radha, *Kundalini Yoga for the West.*

bowl) then I am free. Accept her as my friend and a formidable power will stir from its sleep. I must be willing to listen.

~

I am glad Swami Radha and I started as friends. Over the years, that basic affection we had for each other became a real sustaining bond during times that were difficult between us. Once during a Straight Walk workshop, she confronted my pride with such ferocity that I was left badly shaken, even though I knew her anger was justified. I had come back from lunch on the first day of the workshop without having made a copy of my summary paper from the exercise she had asked us to do that morning. At the root of my indifference was a petty, adolescent kind of resistance to being told what to do by a woman—a resistance that was almost too infantile to believe possible. Yet I could hear the defiance in my voice when she asked me to read my paper.

"I didn't have time to make a copy," I said.

Without missing a beat her reply came back, sharp and quick.

"That would serve you, wouldn't it?"

I felt the cold, harsh tone of her words penetrate right through me and my face flushed hot with pride. But that didn't stop her. In one of those all-or-nothing moments she confronted my arrogance full force. What about my attachment to my family? My need to have things go my way, my desire to be comfortable—taking the ashram for granted, taking *her* for granted? And then came one example after another. She overlooked nothing, not even those things I was certain I hadn't done, and by the time she was finished my pride had been reduced to a great lump of seething confusion.

Within the next twenty-four hours a higher knowing entered my mind and began to dissolve the pride. A larger perspective entered to take its place. It was like waking up to a clear, soft morning, with the recognition that peace had come during the night without my really knowing how it had come. Lying in bed I again went over the exchange between us, only this time I could hear how much my speech and actions reflected my separation from the Light. Swami Radha had acted fast to save what embers remained. When the time was right I called over to Many Mansions and asked to see her.

"I want to apologize. I had not realized how far the arrogance had taken me away and I'm truly sorry to have been so inconsiderate of you."

She looked at me with deep love and concern in her eyes.

"I took a big chance," she said.

"You did?"

"Yes. You might have left."

I was shocked and felt a need to protest. No, I wanted to say, I wouldn't leave because you challenged me. How could you think that? But I didn't say a word. For the first time I realized how my arrogance could destroy the Light and how hard it is to be the one who has to penetrate that arrogance. For the first time since coming to the path of yoga I had an inkling of what unconditional love is really about.

"There are times," she continued, "when your connection to the Light will be no more than a thin red thread. No matter what happens never let that thread break even if you can't see it. When the dark clouds obscure the sun it doesn't mean that the sun is no longer there."

∼

When Swami Radha gave me a mantra initiation in the mid-1980s she called it a spiritual marriage.

"The mantra will be your protection," she said, "as long as you keep your connection to it."

She had substantial reason for making this claim. In the spring of 1956, a couple of weeks after her return home from India, a man attempted to assault her as she made her way home at night after giving a lecture at the Westmount library in Montreal. She had decided to take a shortcut across the park and wasn't more than halfway across it when she heard heavy footsteps running up to her from behind. Instinctively she slowed her pace, hoping that slowing down would take some of the ardor out of her attacker's lust for conquest. Just as the man caught up to her and was about to grab her coat, she turned and faced him.

"Before you do anything," she said, "I want you to do me a favor."

"What is it?" the man asked. "Is it money you want?"

"No. Just say three words. Om Namah Sivaya. Om Namah Sivaya."

"What language is that?" he demanded.

"Sanskrit...," she started to say, but the man suddenly looked at his watch.

"Oh! I'm late for the bus!" he exclaimed and walked quickly away, leaving her standing on the sidewalk alone and unharmed.

"The amazing thing," she told me, "was that I had been home from India only a few weeks, not enough time to really develop my practice with the mantra. Even so it was already a protection."

It was not long after receiving my initiation into sanyas that I happened to be at the Canada-U.S. border just south of Creston when a man suddenly burst into the Canadian Customs and Immigration office brandishing a semi-automatic pistol.

"Stay where you are and don't move!" he shouted.

It took a few moments for my mind to accept that this was the real thing—an extremely dangerous situation. The gunman was plainly desperate. One of the border guards, acting on a hunch, had gone out to search his car, and within moments uncovered a cache of weapons and ammunition in the trunk. The guard was unarmed, which probably saved his life. Now, however, we were all in it. I watched desperation and rage flash across the gunman's face and the very clear thought entered my mind:

"If this is the end, then I want only the Light filling my mind when I go."

I started repeating the mantra of the Light Invocation silently to myself. The gunman, who had been ranting up to that point, suddenly stopped talking and looked around the room. Finally he spotted a door opening into a large broom closet.

"Get in there!" he barked, waving his gun towards the closet.

Very steadily and carefully the three of us moved together towards the closet door—no sudden moves, no surprises—facing the gunman with every step. Then he said something completely unexpected.

"You could've just let me go, ya dumb jerk!" he bellowed at the guard who had searched his car. "Then I wouldn'a had to do this to ya."

As unlikely as it seems, I'm certain there was a hint of remorse in his voice. For the first time I began to think that we had a chance to survive this.

Once we were in the closet, the gunman slammed the door shut and pushed something big and heavy against it. Then silence, and he was gone.

We waited a full minute to be sure, then the three of us heaved against the door and broke out. Several hours later the man was captured by police after a wild chase through the fields around Creston.

That night I told Swami Radha the details of what had happened at the border. I said I thought the mantra had helped protect us.

"I have no doubt of that," she replied.

~

It was early June 1994. Alicia had finished her third year at McGill University in Montreal and was planning to come home for a few days around the middle of the month before starting a summer job in Vancouver. Swami Radha asked how she was getting on at school, whether she was liking Montreal, what her plans were for the summer, the kinds of questions parents are frequently asked about their children's progress. But Swami Radha and Alicia were good friends. They had known each other a long time. Although the questions may have been simple inquiries, she listened closely to my responses.

"You'd be interested to hear about Alicia's relationship with Tara," I told her. "She's had it for years, developed the connection with Tara entirely on her own without saying anything to anyone. She even bought a tiny little statue of Tara which she takes with her everywhere. And she talks to it. Whenever Alicia is facing a large question in her life she talks to Tara about it, which to me is very interesting because it happened spontaneously, all of its own accord."

Swami Radha nodded and smiled and looked thoughtful. It had been a wonderful night with her and we were all in a pretty high mood. In spite of the arthritis that made physical movement difficult for her, Swami Radha seemed tonight to be particularly animated.

"Gopalananda," she said. "Do you see this?"

She pointed to a Tibetan wool carpet rolled up underneath her desk. It was a beautiful deep-woven burgundy carpet with a dark blue and white border and a series of white mandala patterns aligned along the center. I had admired it many times and told her so.

"Well, I think it must be yours then," she laughed. "You'd better take it with you tonight."

Two weeks later, after Alicia had been home for a few days, she called over from Many Mansions one afternoon around five o'clock to tell me that Swami Radha would like me to drop by and see her when I had some time. Well, I knew that meant as soon as possible, and I quickly washed up and went over to Many Mansions. Swami Radha was seated in her usual favorite chair having a light supper and watching the news on CNN when I walked into the sunroom.

"Oh, you're here. Good. Sit down, sit down," and she pointed to the chair closest to her.

"Now then, I have been thinking about something," she paused to look for the "off" button on the remote control and to have a sip of coffee, a sure sign that something was up. She seemed excited and happy, and very focused.

"I want to know if you would be willing to give Alicia a mantra initiation," she said. "That is what is on my mind. Alicia and I had a little talk about it this afternoon, and she would be very happy to receive an initiation from you. Now if you agree, then the three of us should meet as soon as possible so that everything is clear and we all understand what this is about. So what do you think about that?"

What did I think about that? How could I even begin to find words adequate to describe a moment as sweet as this? My eyes filled with tears and I couldn't speak. How could I? I could not think of another time in my life when I had experienced as much love as this moment had brought. Of course I would be honored to give my daughter an initiation. Of course I must finish what I agreed to do. And that is strictly between me and Alicia and Swami Radha and this sublime Lila that has orchestrated the whole thing. All I could say was thank you.

"So, I think it is time for your supper, now. Maybe after you've eaten, you and Alicia can come over and we'll have a visit and talk about what comes next. This is just great! You see, Gopalananda, it puts your whole relationship with Alicia on a completely different level where it ought to be now. You've done your part and you've done well with her. But now it's time to take it to another level. And I think from what I see that you have gotten something of the mantra in you from your practices, so the time is right for you too. Om Om."

When I bent down to hug her, Swami Radha reached up from her chair, put her arms around my neck and kissed me warmly on the cheek. The Light was brilliant around us.

CHAPTER NINETEEN

Last Meeting

On the spiritual path a wandering mind is a dangerous thing. You never know where it will take you, or where you'll end up." Swami Radha had said those words to me many times. Even so, the last time I saw her I had fallen under the spell of that wandering mind. I was preparing to return to the ashram after several months of working with her on her biographical material and she had asked me to come to see her before leaving. I had every right to expect a difficult meeting. For several weeks I had ignored the signs that my focus on the project was wavering and I had reached the point where I had no idea how to get back to what was real, or even if I wanted to come back. It was a very dangerous place to be.

The problem had developed around an attachment that was still much stronger than I had thought—family and home, or at least what they symbolized. Working with Swami Radha in Spokane had taken me out of the ashram and into a mid-sized city for a period of time that was considerably longer than any previous period away from the ashram.

Each day I would walk the three blocks from Swami Radha's apartment to Radha House for lunch and supper, and gradually, without my being aware of it, my attention was increasingly drawn to the big, old houses along the street and the people I saw living in them. One house I passed each day showed all the signs of being a family home: a basketball hoop over the garage door, a large gangly dog that greeted me enthusiastically every time I walked by, and a lawn that had been trampled into dust by the pounding of many little feet. Occasionally I could catch a glimpse of the family through their kitchen window, the one that looked out onto the street. In time, a sentimental fantasy about family life—one that I had never actually lived—along with a hidden longing to be "normal" caused me to lose perspective and forget the promises I had made. I saw the storm approaching, there had been plenty of warnings, but I refused to wake up. Swami Radha could also see what was happening and she wasn't pleased.

There had been many signs that I was heading into a spiritual crisis. A brief exchange between us a few weeks earlier was one of the clearest ones. Swami Radha had come across the hall in her wheelchair to the apartment she had given me to use while I wrote the biography script. It was mid-afternoon and she had come to hear the latest section. After I finished reading, she made one or two comments. Then, warming to the subject, she started admonishing me again to bring more of my experience of her teachings into the writing.

"How else will you know?" she asked, imploring me to go deeper. "How else are you going to find out what you really know? Do you think this is going to tell you?" she demanded, pointing to a *New Yorker* magazine sitting on the floor amidst a pile of newspapers and a book of essays by John McPhee. "I doubt it. If it could, you certainly wouldn't need to reflect about anything. No...." A long pause filled the silence and that was that. She nodded to Julie, her assistant, who wheeled her out of the apartment and back across the hall.

After she left I turned and stared at the offending magazine mixed in with all the other magazines and books I'd accumulated since my arrival in Spokane. They weren't the problem; it was the dependency I had put on them, as if they had the power to reveal the secrets of good writing at a single pass. I started to feel as empty and shallow as anything I had read in the past few weeks. Just that morning I had gone to the bookstore, again looking for diversion, distraction—anything to calm the restlessness that had been building in me since the night she had first spoken to me about writing from my own experience. The

New Yorker and I met at the magazine rack like two old friends ecstatic at finding each other again. When, a few minutes later, I stumbled upon a whole shelf of John McPhee books, I couldn't believe my good fortune. Years ago, long before the ashram, I had dreamed of emulating John McPhee's expository prose after I first discovered his essays in the *New Yorker*. Now here they were together under one roof just when I needed them. That was in the morning. A few hours later my spurious confidence crumpled under the piercing glance of Swami Radha's discriminating eye.

In a meeting a few days later, she took up this subject again.

"Many people," she said, as I sat in my usual place across the desk from her, "and you have done it too, read all sorts of stuff—*Scientific American, New Yorker, Harper's*—but they don't deal with anything in their lives. They're not interested enough to find out why they are here. Is it to understand evolution? Do they say, 'Okay, so how do I go about it?' No. They entertain themselves with all sorts of distractions and when I say something about it they don't like it. I saw that when I gave talks at satsang, I'm really not much more than an entertainer to most of the people in the room. If they had the money they'd go somewhere else to be entertained. They're hardly out the door before they're talking about something totally unrelated, and by the time they reach Main House and have coffee or a snack it's all gone. I would not have seen the facts if I had not been clear-eyed. I'd be living in an illusion that I am somehow a tremendous influence on people. Sometimes, yes. But only for a brief while.

"So I have to find out: Who are the ones who have come from the past? Are they from the Tibetan yogini life, or the Kashmiri yogini life, or the Egyptian? You see?" Pause. "You're very careful, Gopalananda. You don't want to say too much, um?"

I certainly didn't. But she had it right—careful. The ego was being very careful.

"I don't think I have very much to say, and I don't know if that's an old habit or an old protection, or even if it's true. All the work I have done in the past has been to get to this point where I can be here and do this work the way I am doing it now, and be sensitive to that. Twelve years ago I came to the ashram with a big load of karma that had to be worked off. I know that now. The dreams pointed it out to me. So I'm in the place right now where a lot of that is done, and I am free now to move to the next place. But I don't know what that looks like or where or how? And when I look at my dreams now, the dreams seem to say, 'Well, you're doing pretty well.' There's some dreams I've had with you that have put me in…brought me very close to you. And I say, 'Yes, that is all true.' But I still don't know who I am, in the sense of what you are saying tonight. I don't have a right idea of that. So when you say things, I listen very carefully here but I don't have any image of who I am in this."

"Well," she said, "once you identify with the Light, you will know. I feel that the photograph* will finally get you there. I think what you're dealing with today is from that time."

She shifted a little in her chair and then continued.

"Take this young woman who came to see me today. She is twenty-seven now, but when she first came to the ashram she was maybe three years old or just turning four. So she has no particular recollection of any events from that time, but over the years she has always had a strong feeling of having once been in a place where everything was happy, everything was beautiful, even though she couldn't remember it exactly. It was years later when her parents talked about it that she remembered something and wanted to come and see me again. So it is a question of what you respond to, and where that response comes from.

"But most of the time you haven't listened. There were moments when you did understand and that created hopes that you would soon understand more. But most of the time your ego or your pride was stronger.

---

* See cover and page 3.

"You see, you also had an interesting name. The biblical David became king mostly by using his wits. But after he had been made king he could not hold onto what he had been given. But now take your last name, Forsee. Can you foresee your mistakes before they happen? Can you foresee the outcome of your decisions? Your actions? Where you are going, what you have in mind, what you want to do? This time you were given a little prod to keep you from repeating your mistakes from the past.

"Once you can identify with the Light—that's where you find your identification—probably then the details will be given to you because you will be strong enough to accept them. You won't end up in a mental hospital, or whatever, like many people who tried to force their Kundalini energy and then couldn't handle what they experienced. But it's not easy. Let me tell you that. It's not easy.

"You have to become much more aware of yourself—as a man, as a son, as a young man, as a student, as a lover, as a husband, as a father, as a salesman, as a flyer, as the logger—all the things that you have done in your life. These personality aspects are all you know about your self from this lifetime. Now if I come along and say to you, 'You have also been a disciple of Abhinavagupta, or you have been an assistant or member of the Kali temple, or you have been one of the twenty-five young men Machig trained in Tibet, or you have been....' Well, what would you do with that? So you have to wait. Simple as that. And, as you seem to have a happy feeling with your connection to the photograph, you just have to relax and go with it. Obviously, there was a time that seemed to have been wonderful for you—ideal—and now the chance has come back again. So we'll see where it is meant to go. And that's it."

"And in the meantime?"

"In the meantime you work on the manuscript, not concerned with the past or what will be in the future. You work with what is at hand. I can see that you are too easily distracted when you are working on something. Maybe you want to be polite or you want to respond to people. But when somebody wants to take you away from your work, can you not say, 'Sorry, but I have a job to do' or 'Can I give you some time later?' "

Fierce pride and a distracted mind. Swami Radha had reached the heart of the matter. At the very end of our time that night, just as I was getting up to leave, she wondered if perhaps I still had a little pride hidden. The answer soon became evident.

Swami Radha had the courage to offend pride where pride threatened to undermine my resolve to go towards the Light. I had been on the receiving end of her courage many times over the years and I had learned long ago that it is the little things in life that draw the roots of pride out into the Light. Swami Radha didn't pursue the issue of hidden pride after that. She didn't have to. In almost no time at all the issue came to the fore on its own and this time she went after it.

"When are you going to do something about the rings you left on my Chinese desk?"

It wasn't immediately evident to everyone in the room who she was actually addressing or what desk she was talking about. But I knew. I felt the heat rising in my face and a slight band of tension crossing my eyes and forehead as the pride rushed to the surface. My ears started to ring. Pride, no longer restrained by reason, reflection, or even simple consideration for her, rushed headlong into the fire of its own making.

"I did not put the coffee rings on your desk. That is not how I was brought up."

Awkward silence, pause, she turned away without a word and I was left sitting in the tiny pool of my own juices, isolated and ashamed. It was that quick. Even as I spoke the words I could hear the arrogance in my voice, defending myself against what I perceived to be unjust criticism. What did it matter how the cup rings got there? What mattered was that something she valued had been damaged through carelessness, and could I fix it. The tension across my eyes heralded intentional blindness, ringing ears obliterated hearing, and the principle of obedience (or even basic consideration) flew out the window. Pride had risen up like an angry serpent—fast, destructive, unthinking, and the damage was done.

A week later I phoned and asked if I could come and fix the desk. "Yes." Pause. "Thank you."

Her words burned into me. No. It is not you who must thank me. It is I who must thank you for giving me another chance. Forgiving me. Forgiving, and thus overwhelming the tyranny of pride, using the weapon of loving kindness. That is what she did over and over until the job was done.

~

I arrived for our last meeting about one o'clock just as she was finishing her lunch. Except for the daylight pouring through the window by the desk, everything was pretty much as it had always been the nights I had come to read to her. She was sitting at her desk in the black swivel chair that had always seemed to me to be too large for her tiny frail body. It was one of the few chairs she could sit in comfortably as she endured the arthritis that was slowly claiming her physical body in the last months of her life. Her attention, as usual, was focused on the work directly in front of her. I walked to the desk, pranamed, and waited. Silently, without looking up, she gestured for me to sit in the chair across from her.

"Why are you here at this time of day? It's not the best time for me right now."

Her voice sounded edgy and sharp.

"I didn't want to be late in coming to see you."

"Mm. Well, you're here. See if you can help out with the books or whatever is needed. I am going to lie down now. Julie or someone will call over to Radha House when I am up."

Our meeting was over. I got up, pranamed again, and left the room straight away. Outside, the heat of the day closed in around me. It was hard to breathe. I felt very unhappy and slightly ill as I made my way to Radha House three blocks away.

The afternoon passed and no one phoned for me. I felt completely isolated, a nonentity sitting at the dining table while people I had known and even loved as recently as that morning passed by without a word or even a smile. They had real things to do, duties to attend to, a place to live, a purpose for living—all anyone could ask for. I did not feel grateful to anyone or anything, which was a sure sign of the despair I was feeling. Supper came and went but I have no memory of it except making sure that I took long enough washing the dishes for everyone to go so that I could be alone again. I finished the dishes in silence, sat down, and waited some more. A newsmagazine beckoned at my elbow but I turned away and looked out the window instead, searching the garden for signs of life in the looming darkness.

I am an old hand with Swami Radha. What I was going through was very similar to what I had seen happen to others.

"Can you learn from the mistakes of others?" she often asked.

Sitting alone at the table that night, it was painfully evident that I had not even learned from my own mistakes, let alone anyone else's. Around 8:30 that evening the phone rang.

"You can come over now," the voice said.

I hung up and started to gather up my things. Protracted delay had worn out my anxiety; I just wanted to get it over with and be gone.

CHAPTER TWENTY

Field of Silence

In the field of silence is the power of speech realized.

Two days after I awakened with this dream fragment echoing in my mind, Swami Radha died peacefully at home in Spokane, after a long, painful siege with arthritis. Over the two or three years preceding her death, the disease had slowly ravaged her body until finally it was not possible for her to move without assistance. Even so, she still insisted on getting out of her chair several times a day, and with the help of one of her disciples, she would walk slowly around her apartment or out onto the enclosed sun porch that was built for her in the last year of her life. On good days we would drive downtown to any one of her favorite restaurants, and she would treat us to coffee and ice cream, or something special from the dessert menu. She loved taking people out like this, partly to show them that spiritual life didn't have to be so intensely serious all the time, but also because it took her mind away from the pain of the arthritis. She also wanted to stay alert to the tastes and trends that were being expressed through the small daily events in the life around her.

Swami Radha had always been curious and interested in life. From the time she was a little girl to the very last hours of her life she wanted to know, and she used whatever Krishna presented her with to keep doing the work she had promised to do. That was her nature and her purpose for living, and at the time of her death not one strand of unfinished business remained for someone else to clear up. The end was precisely in accord with how she had lived her whole life. What did remain was her indomitable spirit and the promises she had extracted from her close devotees in the last year of her life.

They say in the East that the yogi or yogini knows the time of his or her death. Swami Radha must have known, so precise had been her preparation for departure, so clear had been the signs that she would soon be leaving us. Even I knew. Although I had not seen her for two months, somehow I knew. A week before she died, I spontaneously started writing about my early experiences around death and dying, though why I had felt compelled at that time to recall these events was a mystery. For me it was just a way of entering into the task of reviewing my life, something that Swami Radha had urged me to do during my last visit with her.

"Go through your diaries," she had said. "Find out what is there, what you really know, what your experience has been. Find out what your duty is, and do it!" Over and over during that last visit, she had said, "Think things through, think things through. Make a plan and stick to it. I want to see what your plan is going to be."

After our last conversation, it was clear to me that I had taken her for granted, that I had been taking the Divine for granted, with the result that my mind had drifted into a kind of closed circle of gratification which had weakened it and caused me to lose my direction. In spite of that, Swami Radha hung onto me. In spite of the fact that the thin red thread connecting us had been frayed by my neglect, still she hung onto me. In the meantime I reviewed my diaries, and before long the myriad images and impressions of daily life recorded over many years began to flow together into a picture that made sense and revealed a purpose for my life that I have known deep within myself for a long time. How easy it had been to become distracted, forget, and finally lose my way. How hard it was to admit that I was lost and needed her help to find my way back again. And yet, through the silence that had come between us after our last meeting, it was the Light that illumined my way back to her. Without it I would have disappeared forever.

Diary Notes from the Journey Back

Read the diaries. Mark everything she has said to me. If I have her in my mind, that will crowd out all the negative influences.

Stunned by a phone call from an old friend I knew in high school over thirty years ago. How did she find me? Why is she calling now? She tells me that she has two grown-up daughters and no husband, divorced after twenty years of marriage. She has just moved to the west coast. She would love to see me if I ever come to town. God, why is this happening to me now?

I'm starting to ask myself, What is so absorbing about emotions? What benefits have I received from being emotional? The best I can come up with is attention. Being emotional is a way of getting attention. I'm wondering if there is some desire left in my old memory that is not available to me now. Final question: What do I invite by my interest into the temple of my mind? What indeed.

Awake early this morning. Want to go. Want to sleep in. Wanting my way, my own time, my own schedule, my own everything—and resenting Swami Radha because she is ignoring me. The selfishness of my ego is boundless. I go to chant in the Temple. Mind clears and I see the antidote for now: BE HERE! Use the mantra for building concentration. Mind resists, wanders off. Come back through listening. Wanders again. Re-

peat. Come back…until finally mind is enmeshed in mantra and all the negativity floats away. It works. The mantra works. I tell myself I will see her again only when I have been victorious.

A message from Swami Radha today, delivered by one of her devotees. "Tell Gopalananda not to use up so much paper when he's faxing." I slump hearing this. Become sullen and defiant. I forgot that I could have said "Thank you" instead. "Thank you for having enough interest in me to be concerned about what I am doing." It is my first contact with her since our last meeting. The Divine is deadly serious this time.

Mornings are all the same now. I awaken with a dull, running commentary on my separation from Swami Radha and how I'm trying to bridge back to wholeness, trying to connect to her again. But it's hard. My pride doesn't want to let that happen. Where is the Light? Where has my Light gone? How did it go? When did it happen? Will it ever come back?

For the first time in weeks, I awaken peacefully. My mind is calm. I feel peaceful and rested. I want to hang onto this feeling but it doesn't seem possible, though I am grateful for the temporary relief it affords. Also I begin to see a plan taking shape. My mind is busy with thoughts about the writing, about building a base of understanding from my own record.

How do I know you care, Divine Mother? Do you accept me even now? Am I incapable of caring for you? Is it true what Swami Radha said, that some people love their pride so much they're incapable of loving anything else? I wonder if I can learn how to love. Small steps make the right beginning. I never thought dryness and shattered illusions would hurt so much. What am I being called upon to sacrifice?

I'm stunned to see an entry in my first diary, August 11, 1979, that tells me I not only have a desire to write well, but that I would like to be able to write "…in the style of New Yorker essayist, John McPhee." A thought form floating in the ocean of my mind for fifteen years before it surfaced at Auntie's bookstore in Spokane and helped to precipitate my fall from grace.

Thinking this morning about the principle difference between my guru and other teachers. She never tried to cajole, or persuade, or convince me through the force of her personality. She took the more difficult route of entering into the situations that could either teach me or destroy me. The point is that what I learn myself is true knowledge. I can try to behave according to how others think I should act, and would willingly do so, particularly if I like the other person or want their approval. But that is not the same as learning from my own keen desire to know and evolve. The route of direct participation is more difficult for Swami Radha, but she does not incur unnecessary karma in the process.

Living in my mind these days is like sitting in a darkened cinema in mid-afternoon on a sunny day, or wandering through a shopping mall wondering why I am there. Either way, it's not very inspiring.

Gopalananda, fill yourself with her material, her transcripts. Keep going. Do not quit. If my actions do not reflect the highest standards in myself, then the discipline, the path itself, is called into question. Put Gopalananda into the Light and let David become his servant, his friend. I'm praying hard, these days, that my mind will return to Krishna and Mother Radha. Right now prayer is the only thing I have left.

Remembrance Day. Charles returns from his visit with Swami Radha in Spokane. He says to me, "Swami Radha told me to tell you that the plant you gave her is doing well." I ask Charles to repeat the message because I'm barely able to believe I heard it right. I had given her the little plant the first day I arrived in Spokane to start the video project. So much has happened since then and the little plant has perked away through it all. I had forgotten my gift to her.

"In the field of silence is the power of speech realized." A dream fragment; it's all I remember. Mind is unruly and lacking focus this morning. What is stirring it up?

Swami Radha died this morning at five o'clock. Apparently it was quite sudden. Her heart stopped. Last night she had stayed up and watched her favorite opera, Turandot. She loved the strength of the tenor parts, especially Vinchero! Victory!

Swami Radhananda and I went to Spokane this morning to bring her body home to the ashram. Crossing the border coming back into Canada, we are met by a magnificent double rainbow arching across the western sky. Radha and Krishna, Radha and Gurudev. Hari Om.

Tonight I found an envelope in my mailbox. It was from Swami Radha. Someone was supposed to have delivered it last week but forgot. It's fat. My hands shake as I open it. Inside are four photographs of her taken in Montreal in 1954.

In the photos she is wearing the jeweled peacock feather crown of Lord Krishna and her hands form the mudra of Krishna playing the flute. She is dressed in a blue-green Indian dance costume that appears to be made of silk. Her eyes and mouth reflect a kind of mischievous twinkle, just like Krishna's.

The little note she included with the photos was addressed to me. She signed it "Love, Mataji."

So it is true. In the field of silence lie the seeds of Realization.

Epilogue

Again I recall Swami Radha's words to me late that night in her apartment in Spokane.

"Go back to your diaries," she had said, her voice firm in the conviction of her own experience. "Read what's there. You must be able to see how far you've come."

It has been an extraordinary process reviewing almost twenty years of day-to-day life on a spiritual path. She was right. Progress along a spiritual path cannot be measured by conventional milestones. The Divine does not sweeten the return on my investment with an annual bonus or a letter of commendation. So it has to be something else that encourages me to keep going along this arduous path of renunciation, some way of measuring, some way of remembering.

In moments of stillness I have seen the Light and have heard the sound of Krishna's flute. I know because my diaries reveal the Light running like a thin golden thread through my years with Swami Radha. And yet I forget. Caught up in an old personality aspect, I forget. When this happens I must turn again to the reflective process and the people around me who care.

An example. Within hours of finishing this book, I was swept by self-doubt. What will people think? Did I accomplish *anything?* Will anyone understand or even care? The tyranny of self-doubt undermines this journey's progress in the absence of precise memory. And what memory is precise? That is why Swami Radha was so emphatic. I have to know what my experience has been, how far I have come, in order to protect myself against an ego that will use anything, even doubt, to claim the throne of Higher Consciousness for itself.

And so I started again with a few key words to identify where I was and what was happening: completion, doubt, focus, what's next.

I reflect and the question comes: What's real in this play of emotions? I remember Swami Radha telling us how much trepidation she felt subjecting her deepest, most cherished spiritual experiences to public scrutiny in the *Radha* book* and then doing it anyway for the benefit of those who might be inspired enough to take a stand for their own spiritual evolution. I continue, and my reflections take me to the fact that it was Swami Radha who showed me how to make sense of my life through having a spiritual focus. My writing is an acknowledgment of that fact and therefore my stand will be tested.

My eyes are drawn to Shakti Lakini, goddess of the third chakra in the Kundalini system. She holds fire in one hand and a bolt of lightning in the other. Lakini is not just raw emotion. She is a Vajra-dakini, meaning that feminine power that cuts through illusion with fiery passion.

"You cannot be lukewarm on this path," Swami Radha often said. "Lukewarm gets you nowhere."

Whenever Swami Radha cut through my clouded thinking with her flashes of insight, fear and doubt would bolt like a startled ram. The wisdom gained from experience of her is real. I must *see* where I have come from.

Now I do the Divine Light Invocation and put the issue of what comes next into the Light. To my surprise an image of the little rose book** rising out of a pool of water appears in the Light, along with the memory of a letter Swami Radha wrote to Swami Sivananda in Decem-

* Swami Sivananda Radha, *Radha: Diary of a Woman's Search.*
** See Swami Sivananda Radha, *The Rose Ceremony.*

ber 1955 from Dehra Dun. The letter described a little ritual she had created in gratitude to Swami Sivananda for the deep spiritual awakening that had come to her through the dance training he had arranged for her to take in Dehra Dun. As part of the ritual she took an orange-colored rose from the garden where she was staying and taking the petals from the rose she placed them one by one into a pool of water, making each one an offering to her guru. Finally, when only the stem of the rose was left, she placed that in the water too, not wanting to keep anything for herself. The message of the rose coming back to me in the Light is clear: make everything I do an offering in gratitude for her.

∽

This morning I walk through thick wet snow on my way to early morning chanting in the temple. By mid-morning the early winter sun will have absorbed my footprints and all traces of my temple visit will have vanished. Near the temple entrance a late fall mushroom pokes its head through the snow, defying the encroaching winter and inevitable death.

"Proud plant," I laugh softly to myself. "I thought you at least would know when to yield and when to resist."

I think about the life force and about will and the choices I have made, and how those choices led me step by step to the entrance of this beautiful little temple. Swami Radha often encouraged me to look back at all the ways Divine Mother had tried to show me my destiny and purpose for this life, and how much I had been protected along the way.

"You will see that many times you were protected from the repercussions of your own ignorance and stubbornness," she said. "But you may also catch a glimpse of who you really are and who you have been all along."

Swami Radha (1911–1995)

Swami Radha was a remarkable woman for our time. Initiated into sanyas in 1956 at the age of 44, she returned to the West at the request of her guru, Swami Sivananda of Rishikesh, and devoted the remainder of her life to updating the ancient Teachings of Yoga. Swami Radha used her manifest life experience as the basis of her teaching, which was noted for its practical relevance to daily living in the West. There was no separation between her life and the teachings of yoga. At the time of her death at the age of 84 she was considered to be one of this century's great spiritual teachers in the ancient tradition of Kundalini Yoga.

Swami Radha founded Yasodhara Ashram, a thriving spiritual community in Canada, and the Association for the Development of Human Potential (ADHP) in the United States. She also established many urban centers, called Radha Houses, in Canada, the United States, Mexico and England.

David Forsee (1944–)

Born in Toronto, David Forsee graduated from Wilfred Laurier University
with a B.A. in English Literature. He
worked as a CBC radio journalist both
in the eastern Arctic and in Ontario.
In the 1970s he developed a business
as an independent trucking con-
tractor in northern Ontario, where he
married and lived with his wife and
their daughter.

David first met Swami Radha at
her ashram in 1979. Following the three-month Yoga Development
Course in 1982, he moved with his family to the ashram and has been
actively engaged in Swami Radha's work ever since. In 1991 he took an
initiation into sanyas (the path of renunciation and selfless service) to
become Swami Gopalananda.

Over the years he developed a close relationship with Swami Radha
as a devotee and friend, and in the latter years of her life worked
closely with her on the production of *Radha's Story,* her video biography. This led to her request that he write this book to discover what he
had learned from their relationship. Swami Gopalananda is on the Board
of Directors of Yasodhara Ashram and on the Editorial Board, which
oversees the continuing publication of Swami Radha's work. He is the
editor of *Ascent,* the ashram's quarterly journal. He teaches at the ashram
and also travels to present Swami Radha's teachings to a wider audience. *Can You Listen to a Woman* is his first book.

Your support for the Yasodhara Ashram's Youth Program is very much appreciated . . .

Your purchase of this book has just helped a participant in the Ashram's Youth Program. How? All proceeds from the sale of *Can You Listen to a Woman* will be donated to the program.

The focus of the program is to help young people between the ages of 18 and 28 bring quality and awareness into their life through the integrated practices of yoga. Participants in the Youth Program are given the opportunity for learning how to live, work, and study in a spiritual community. They are taught how to use the tools of yoga to reflect on their ideals and develop options for realizing their potential in this lifetime.

One of the main tools for reflection is the practice of Karma Yoga, the yoga of work as selfless service. Karma Yoga treats work as a reflection of mind and as such allows one to bring the ideals of yoga into practical daily application. Karma Yoga gives the youth a practical spiritual foundation for their life in the world. For many participants, the Youth Program is a preparation for taking their next step in life.

Yasodhara Ashram is a yoga retreat center and spiritual community dedicated to the teachings of its founder, Swami Sivananda Radha. For information about the Youth Program or about the many courses, retreat programs, and workshops offered at the Ashram, please contact:

Yasodhara Ashram
Box 9, Kootenay Bay, B.C.
V0B 1X0 Canada
(800) 661-8711
FAX: (250) 227-9494
e-mail yashram@netidea.com
or visit us on the web at:
www.yasodhara.org